C000227342

Nine Steps

An ISO 27001:2013 Implementation Overview

Third edition

Nine Steps to Success

An ISO 27001:2013 Implementation Overview

Third edition

ALAN CALDER

IT Governance Publishing

Every possible effort has been made to ensure that the information contained in this book is accurate at the time of going to press, and the publisher and the author cannot accept responsibility for any errors or omissions, however caused. Any opinions expressed in this book are those of the author, not the publisher. Websites identified are for reference only, not endorsement, and any website visits are at the reader's own risk. No responsibility for loss or damage occasioned to any person acting, or refraining from action, as a result of the material in this publication can be accepted by the publisher or the author.

Apart from any fair dealing for the purposes of research or private study, or criticism or review, as permitted under the Copyright, Designs and Patents Act 1988, this publication may only be reproduced, stored or transmitted, in any form, or by any means, with the prior permission in writing of the publisher or, in the case of reprographic reproduction, in accordance with the terms of licences issued by the Copyright Licensing Agency. Enquiries concerning reproduction outside those terms should be sent to the publisher at the following address:

IT Governance Publishing
IT Governance Limited
Unit 3, Clive Court
Bartholomew's Walk
Cambridgeshire Business Park
Ely, Cambridgeshire
CB7 4EA
United Kingdom

www.itgovernance.co.uk

The author has asserted the rights of the author under the Copyright, Designs and Patents Act, 1988, to be identified as the author of this work.

First published in the United Kingdom in 2005
by IT Governance Publishing: ISBN: 978-1-90535-612-6

Second edition published in 2013
ISBN: 978-1-84928-510-0

Third edition published in 2016
ISBN: 978-1-84928-823-1

ABOUT THE AUTHOR

Alan Calder is the founder and executive chairman of IT Governance Ltd (*www.itgovernance.co.uk*), an information, advice and consultancy firm that helps company boards tackle IT governance, risk management, compliance and information security issues. He has many years of senior management experience in the private and public sectors.

The company operates websites around the world that distribute a range of books, tools and other publications on IT governance, risk management, compliance and information security.

CONTENTS

Introduction..1
    The ISO 27000 family 7
    Before you start..9
Chapter 1: Project Mandate..............................13
    Strategic alignment 15
    Prioritisation and endorsement 16
    Change management...17
    The CEO's role 18
    The Project Mandate 20
Chapter 2: Project Initiation..............................27
    Objectives 27
    Project management...28
    Project leadership..28
    Senior management support...............................29
    Project team 31
    Project plan 37
    Structured approach to implementation...........38
    Phased approach..39
    The project plan 40
    Integration with existing security management systems 41
    Quality system integration 42
    Looking ahead...43
    Costs and project monitoring 43
    Risk register 44
Chapter 3: ISMS Initiation..................................47
    Continual improvement 47
    Security improvement plan 48
    Expanding the RACI matrix 48
    Documentation..48

Contents

Four levels of documentation 51
Documentation approaches 51

Chapter 4: Management Framework **55**
Scoping 56
Endpoint security 58
Defining boundaries 60
Network mapping 62
Cutting corners 63
Formalise key arrangements 64
Information security policy 65
Communication strategy 66
Staff buy-in 68

Chapter 5: Baseline Security Criteria **71**

Chapter 6: Risk Management **73**
Introduction to risk management 74
Baseline security controls 76
Risk assessment 76
Five-step risk assessment process 77
Risk workshop 79
Impacts 79
Controls 80
Risk assessment tools 81
Controls 81
Nature of controls 82
Control selection criteria 84
Statement of applicability 86
Risk treatment plan 87

Chapter 7: Implementation **89**
Competencies 89
The 'all persons' requirement 90
Staff awareness 91
Outsourced processes 93

Contents

Chapter 8: Measure, Monitor and Review 95
Internal audit, and testing..96
Management review...99
Chapter 9: Certification **101**
ISO 27001 Resources **105**
ITG Resources..**125**

INTRODUCTION

Cyber risk has become a critical business issue, with senior management increasingly under pressure – from customers, regulators and partners – to ensure their organisation can defend against, respond to and recover from cyber attack.

Resilience against cyber attack requires an organisation to do more than just erect digital defences; a significant percentage of successful attacks originate in the analogue, physical world, or are aided and exacerbated by physical and environmental vulnerabilities. Effective cyber security therefore requires a comprehensive, systematic and robust information security management system; boards, customers and regulators all seek assurance that information risks have been identified and are being managed.

The international standard ISO/IEC 27001:2013 *Information technology – Security techniques – Information security management systems – Requirements* is the blueprint for managing information security in line with an organisation's business, contractual and regulatory requirements, and its risk appetite. Information security has always been an international issue and this version of the Standard reflects eight years of improvements in the understanding of effective information security management. It also takes account of the evolution in the cyber threat landscape over that period and allows for a wide range of best practice controls.

Information security is now clearly also a management issue, a governance responsibility. The design and implementation of an information security management system (ISMS) is a management role, not a technological one.

It requires the full range of managerial skills and attributes, from project management and prioritisation through communication, sales skills and motivation to delegation, monitoring and discipline. A good manager who has no technological background or insight can lead a successful ISMS implementation, but without management skills, the most technologically sophisticated information security expert will fail at the task.

This is particularly so if the organisation wants to derive maximum, long term business value from the implementation of an ISMS. Achieving external certification is increasingly a standard cost of doing business; achieving the level of information security awareness and good internal practice that enables an organisation to safely surf the stormy, cruel seas of the information age requires a level of culture change no less profound than that required to shift from industrial to post-industrial operations.

I know all this because my background is as a general manager, not as a technologist. I came to information security in 1995 because I was concerned about the information security exposures faced by a company of which I was CEO. When you're the CEO, and you're interested in it, you can make an ISMS happen – as I've proved a number of times. While this book will shorten the learning curve for other CEOs in my position, it's really aimed at the manager – often an IT or information security manager, sometimes a quality manager – who is charged with tackling an ISO 27001 implementation and who wants to understand the route to a positive outcome. It builds on the experience of many ISO 27001 implementations and reflects the nine step implementation methodology that now underpins all the ISO 27001 products and services that can be accessed through IT Governance Ltd, the company I founded back in 2005.

These nine steps work in any organisation – public sector, voluntary sector or private – anywhere in the world. Technology infrastructure, business model, organisational architecture and regulatory requirements all inform the context for implementation of an ISO 27001 ISMS but don't limit its applicability. We've helped implement an ISO 27001 ISMS in businesses with as few as two people, in mammoth, multi-country global enterprises, and in organisations of all sizes and types in between.

The second-biggest challenge that, in my experience, is faced by information security technologists everywhere in the world is getting – and keeping – the board's attention. The biggest challenge is gaining – and maintaining – the organisation's *interest in* and *application to* the project. Ongoing press and public attention regarding cyber risk is driving the issue onto board agendas and, when boards do finally understand they need to act – systematically and comprehensively – against information security threats, they become very interested in hearing from their information security specialists. They even develop an appetite for investing organisational dollars into hardware and software solutions, and for mandating the development of a new ISMS – or the tightening up of an existing one.

A successful ISMS project stems from and depends on genuine top management support. Progress is quicker if the project is seen as having a credible business need: to win an outsourcing or other customer contract, for instance, or to comply with a public funding requirement, improve competitiveness or reduce regulatory compliance costs and exposures.

When we first decided to tackle information security, way back in 1995, my organisation was required to achieve both

ISO 9001 certification and Investor in People (IiP) recognition as a condition of its branding and trading licence. We also intended to sell information security and environmental management services and – out of a desire to practice what we preached, as well as from a determination to achieve the identifiable benefits of tackling all these components of our business – we decided to pursue both BS 7799 and ISO 14001 at the same time.

BS 7799 certification only existed then in an unaccredited form and was, essentially, a Code of Practice. There was only one part to it and, while certification was technically not possible, some Certification Bodies were interested in issuing statements of conformity. The other standards that we were interested in did all exist but, at that time, it was generally expected that an organisation would approach each standard on its own, developing standalone manuals and processes. This was hardly surprising, as it was unusual for any organisation to pursue more than one standard at any time!

We made the momentous decision to approach the issue from primarily a business perspective, rather than a quality one. We decided that we wanted to create a single, integrated management system that would work for our business, and that was capable of achieving multiple certifications. While this seemed to fly in the face of standard practice around management system implementation, it seemed to be completely in line with the spirit of the standards themselves.

We also decided that we wanted everyone in the organisation to take part in the process of creating and developing the integrated management system that we envisioned. We believed that was the fastest and most certain way of getting them to become real contributors to the project, both in the short and long term. We used external consultants for part of the ISO 9001 project but there simply was no BS 7799 expertise available externally.

This lack of BS 7799 experts was a minor challenge compared with the lack of useful books or tools. Today, you can purchase books such as *An Introduction to ISO27001 and Information Security*; back then there were bookshelves full of thick, technologically-focused books on all sorts of information security issues, but nothing that might tell a business manager how to systematically implement an information security management system. We had no option but to try to work it out for ourselves.

We actually did the job twice, once under the unaccredited scheme and the second time after the Standard had become a two-parter and had been accredited (the earlier, single part had become a Code of Practice and a new part, a specification for an information security management system, had been introduced). In fact, our accredited audit was also our certification body's first observed audit for its own UKAS accreditation. While that was an interesting experience, it did mean that our systems had to be particularly robust if they were to stand the simultaneous scrutiny of two levels of external auditors!

We underwent external examination on five separate occasions within a few months and our integrated management system achieved all the required external certifications and recognitions. We did this without anything more than the part time assistance of one ISO 9001 consultant and an internal quality management team of one person. Steve Watkins, now a director of IT Governance Ltd and a UKAS Technical Assessor for ISO 27001, was that quality manager, and he did most of the real work to create our integrated, multi-standard management system. Admittedly, the organisation was a relatively small one but, although we only employed about 80 people (across three sites), we did also have an associate consultant team that was nearly a hundred strong. And back then, we probably couldn't have done something as complex as this in a much larger organisation.

The lessons that Steve and I learned in our first two implementations – and our experience with ISO 27001 implementations since then, often in very substantial public and private sector organisations – has enabled us to crystallise the nine keys to a successful ISMS implementation.

Properly managed and led, any ISO 27001 project can be successful. We've proved it.

Over the years, my organisation (IT Governance Ltd: *www.itgovernance.co.uk*) has developed approaches to implementing an ISMS that can help project managers identify and overcome many of the very real problems they face in achieving a successful outcome. We've also developed unique tools and techniques that simplify the process, that fit together around the nine steps described in this book, and that enable organisations to succeed without additional external assistance. Information security success, in the long term, does not need to be consultant-dependent; it does depend on the organisation itself. This book describes the key issues, the building blocks of success, and tells you how to tackle them.

The book is intended to be a fairly high-level guide to the nine-step implementation process and it therefore refers, from time to time, to more detailed books or tools that have been developed or published by my company. In particular, it often makes reference to the substantially more detailed and comprehensive *IT Governance – An International Guide to Data Security and ISO27001/ISO27002, Sixth Edition*, which Steve and I originally wrote to fill the evident gap in available guidance on the subject. That book is also now The Open University's postgraduate text book on information security.

In each case where I have made a specific reference, the book or tool is unique and was developed to do the specific job that I describe it as doing. We developed these books, tools and services because there simply was nothing available on the market that did a comparable job or that delivered the sort of return on investment that we know our customers are looking for.

The ISO 27000 family

The information security Standard is, in fact, a two-part standard which has undergone considerable evolution. One part of the Standard (ISO 27001:2013) provides a specification for the ISMS (it uses words like 'shall', particularly in Annex A, which is the list of controls). The other part (ISO 27002:2013) has the status of a Code of Practice; the assembled guidance on best practice information security from around the world.

The difference between a specification and a Code of Practice, in the world of management systems standards, is that a specification contains the word 'shall' and specifies what is mandatory for a system if it is to comply with the standard, while a Code of Practice provides guidance and uses words like 'should' to indicate that compliance is not mandatory. Organisations can choose controls from this Code of Practice or anywhere else, provided the requirements of the specification are met. Accredited certification takes place against a requirements specification, not a Code of Practice.

ISO 27001 is linked to ISO 27002 and, where the organisation uses the Annex A controls, ISO 27002 provides the guidance on how to implement those controls.

These two standards are supported by ISO 27000, which provides the definitions on which they rely. This is a lightweight work, but contains useful guidance and all the essential definitions that will help ensure everyone involved in the implementation project is on the same page.

You need to obtain, and study, copies of both *ISO/IEC 27001:2013* and *ISO/IEC 27002:2013*. It is against ISO 27001 specifically that compliance will be measured and the exact words in that Standard have precedence over any other guidance or commentary. Copies of the Standards can be obtained from your national standards body or from *www.itgovernance.co.uk* (IT Governance Ltd is an authorised standards distributor for a number of standards bodies).

In cases of doubt or uncertainty, your certification auditor will refer to the Standards for clarification; if everything you do can be tied down to specific words in the Standard you will be in a strong position. On the other hand, don't assume that if you do something the Standard does not specify your action is incorrect. The Standard is a *minimum* requirement, not a maximum one.

Links to other standards

ISO 27001 is supported by a family of related best practice standards, each of which provides additional guidance on a specific aspect of information security management. This family of standards is continuously growing and developing; up-to-date information is available from *www.itgovernance.co.uk/iso27000-family.aspx*.

ISO 27001:2013 will harmonize with ISO 9001:2015 and ISO 14001:2015, as well as with ISO 22301, ISO 20000-1 and ISO 50001, so that management systems can be effectively integrated.

ISO 27001 implicitly recognises that information security and an ISMS should form an integrated part of any internal control system created as part of corporate governance procedures. The Standard fits in with the approach adopted in the UK by the FRC Guidance on Risk Management.

There is further discussion on the relationships with these other standards, more detail on the interrelationship with ISO 27002, and initial guidance on how frameworks such as ITIL (and ISO 20000) and COBIT could be used in an ISO 27001 implementation in *An Introduction to ISO27001 and Information Security*.

Before you start

It would be worth getting appropriate training before you start your ISMS project.

The most useful training courses are those that provide an introduction to the whole subject, those that cover implementation and those that cover audit. All good courses are accredited by an external examination board, such as IBITGQ (the International Board for IT Governance Qualifications – *www.ibitgq.org*).

An ISO27001 ISMS Foundation Course is a one-day course that provides a broad awareness of the subject and is suitable for all project team members.

An ISO27001 Lead Implementer Course is the ideal course for those who will be responsible for taking the project forward. This is a three-day course that provides practical guidance on effective implementation. The Certified Information Security Lead Implementer (CIS LI) qualification is widely recognised, and CIS LI courses and exams reflect the nine-step approach that I describe.

All management systems have to be subject to internal (management) audit, and a Lead ISMS (or, possibly, an Internal ISMS) Auditor Course will provide those inside your organisation who will be charged with designing and managing your internal information security audit process with the skills they need to do this effectively.

You can see more detailed information about these, and other, courses here: *www.itgovernance.co.uk/itg-training-courses.aspx*. These qualifications can be achieved by attending either a classroom (daily travel or hotel expenses) or a live online (make your own drinks and meals) course.

Training will also, of course, be an important facilitator of the types of changes your organisation may need to make in terms of information security management. Exposing the whole project team to the principles of ISO 27001 through an ISO 27001 Foundation training course is a sensible step after you've provided for the critical lead implementer and lead auditor training. Staff throughout the business will also need specific training in those aspects of security policy that will affect their day-to-day work. The IT manager and IT staff will all need specific competencies in Information Security (see ISO 27001

Clause 7.2) and, if this needs to be enhanced by training, it should be delivered by an organisation that recognises and understands the technical aspects of ISO 27001 training. More information about appropriate training can be found here: *www.itgovernance.co.uk/itg-training-courses.aspx*.

CHAPTER 1: PROJECT MANDATE

It may be something of a cliché but, for information security management system (ISMS) projects, it is certainly true to say that 'well begun is half-way done'. The person charged with leading an ISO/IEC 27001:2013 ISMS project has to reduce something that looks potentially complex, difficult and expensive in terms of time and resources, to something that everyone believes can be achieved in the time frame allocated and with the resources allowed. And then you have to make sure that it is actually delivered!

What this actually means is that the ISMS project leader has to set up the project in such a way that it is adequately resourced, that there is enough time (including for everything that may go wrong) and that everyone understands the risks in the project and accepts the controls that are being deployed to minimise them.

Almost everyone dislikes change. Very few people relish dealing with the unknown. Most people will see an ISMS project as something that brings both change and the unknown into their working life, and not everyone will welcome it. That's normal; they'll get on board in the end.

The project leader, in the first phase of the project, is the person to whom everyone else in the organisation turns for insight, comfort and support. You have to be the person who provides enthusiasm, certainty and an understanding of what's involved.

This means that learning on the job in a transparent fashion is not advisable. I don't mean that you need to know all the answers at the outset, because that's not realistic. As long as you have a clear understanding of the strategic issues and practical knowledge of where to turn for advice and guidance, you can be effective – even if you're only a day or two ahead of everyone else in the detailed knowledge required for the project.

You'd be surprised at the number of times someone has kicked off an ISMS project without adequate preparation, has failed to answer a series of questions or challenges about specific issues adequately, and has then been surprised that the project has lost credibility rather quickly.

Your CEOs support for the project is even more important than your own understanding of what you're trying to achieve. Information security is both a management and a governance issue. Successful implementation of an ISMS depends absolutely on the project having real support from the top of the organisation. With it, you have a real chance of success; without it, none at all. *Securing real top management support* – not mere lip service – is key to ISO 27001 success. In this context, I'm not necessarily talking about the CEO of a large, multi-subsidiary organisation; I'm talking about the person who is accountable for the business success or failure of the trading entity that is considering ISO 27001. This could be a trading division, a subsidiary company, a standalone unit or a virtual organisation.

It's important to be clear about the meaning of 'accountable' in this context. I am talking about the person whose job and career ultimately depend on the success of the business entity that is considering ISO 27001; this person does not always occupy the role that is formally 'where the buck stops'. All organisations know exactly where the buck really stops, and this is the person I'm referring to as the CEO in this chapter.

Strategic alignment

The first reason why the CEO has to fully support you and the ISMS project is that it is a business project, not an IT project. It has to be fully aligned with the business model, business strategy and goals, and has to be prioritised for the business and allocated an appropriate level of resources. While the CEO is unlikely to be the ISMS project leader, the only person who can effectively prioritise cyber security is the CEO. No single project leader is in a position to be clear about the organisation's strategic needs and goals but, as this is a strategic project that affects everyone, you need to be 'in the loop' so that you can tailor your own plans to deliver the organisation's business priorities.

You also need to know what the strategic risks faced by the organisation are, and how these are reflected and prioritised in information security risks. There are many possible questions, the answers to which will be critical to your approach and detailed plan. For instance, is the risk of intellectual property theft more significant – with a greater potential impact – than the risk of, for example, a three day business closure? Is regulatory compliance more, or less, important than reducing the cost of sales? Is information security and regulatory compliance going to be important in outsourcing solutions (or, when faced with a choice between a lower cost, but less secure, and a more secure but more expensive outsourcing option, which one will the organisation choose?). How should conflict between the regulatory requirements of two different jurisdictions in which the organisation trades be resolved? What's the trade-off between the operational flexibility that is allowed to subsidiary organisations, and implementation of a minimum, consistent level of information security and IT service reliability? What are the long term plans for specific support services (if they're going to be outsourced, then you're going to approach ISMS implementation differently than if they're staying in-house)? There are many such questions, the answers to which you need to know before you can even start planning; there are many others that will come up in the course of the project.

Prioritisation and endorsement

The second reason you require this level of support is that, without it, the project simply won't happen. It's not enough for the CEO and executive management simply to acknowledge that the project is important. It's not enough that they merely talk about it. It's not enough that you know the organisation's strategic priorities and are able to align the project with the business plan.

If it really is to happen senior management have to be committed, well and truly determined to achieve it. Top management commitment means that the project gets the financial and human resources it needs. It gets the oversight, 'face time' and internal communication headlines it needs. Unless you have this sort of commitment, there are going to be lots of things that people throughout the organisation will see as higher priorities than your project. Of course, there are going to be *some* higher priorities; what you need is clear prioritisation that is understood across the business and is continuously supported by the CEO.

The relative prioritisation of your project needs to be clearly understood. Within that context, it needs to have the firm and uncompromising endorsement of the CEO. By 'endorsement' I mean that, when those occasionally unnecessary internal barriers appear, the words: "This is a project endorsed/mandated by the CEO" should go a long way to overcoming them.

Change management

The third reason you need the CEO's support is that an ISMS project is likely to be a change management project. The implementation of an ISMS is not a low-impact activity. It may require changes to how computer users do a number of things and it also affects aspects of managers' everyday activities. A successful ISMS project is, in other words, a low-key, but nevertheless wide-ranging change management project and the way you approach it has to learn from the experience of successful change management programmes.

There have been many books written about change management. Many of these projects fail to deliver the benefits that have been used to justify the expense of commencing and seeing them through. Successful implementation of an ISMS does not require a detailed, strategic change management programme, particularly not one devised and driven by external consultants. What it does require is complete clarity among senior management, those charged with driving the project forward, and those whose work practices will be affected, as to why the change is necessary, what the end result must look like and why this result is essential. The change management aspects of this are the third reason why the CEO's support and backing is essential: you want him to be setting the example, doing all the things that you're going to want everyone else to be doing.

The fact is that the Standard itself demands this level of support. It will not allow any certification body to certify an ISMS without getting firm evidence that senior management is committed. The reason for this is simple: if commitment is lacking the ISMS will not be adequate; the risks to the organisation will not have been properly recognised or fully addressed; and the strategic business goals and consequent future information security requirements are unlikely to have been considered.

The CEO's role

Ideally, the CEO should be the driving force behind the programme, and achievement of ISO 27001 certification should be a clearly stated goal in the current business plan. The CEO needs to completely understand the strategic issues around IT governance and information security, and the value to the company of successful certification. The CEO has to be able to articulate this to the board and senior management, and to deal with objections and issues that arise. Above all, he or she has to be sufficiently in command of this part of the business plan to be able to keep it on track against its strategic goals.

The chairman and board should give as much attention to monitoring progress against the ISO 27001 implementation plan as they do to monitoring all the other key business goals. Clause 5.1 of the Standard specifically requires evidence of this commitment from the top: "Top management shall demonstrate leadership and commitment with respect to the information security management system". If the CEO, chairman and board are not behind this project there is little point in proceeding; certification will not happen without clear evidence of such a commitment. This principle of leadership from the top is, of course, also essential to all major change projects.

If you are already the CEO of the organisation, then you're doing exactly the right thing by reading this book and preparing to drive the information security project yourself. If you're not the CEO, then you've got to secure the sort of commitment and support that I described above.

The ideal leader of an ISMS project is a business leader – a COO (chief operations officer) or a line of business leader; adopting an ISMS is a business project and business leadership is therefore fundamental to its success. It is often the case that an ISMS project fails because it has apparently been set up as a technology project and it is therefore seen and treated as a narrow project that doesn't deserve full business commitment. 'Just another IT project' is the wrong message for driving an ISMS into the culture of the organisation.

There are, of course, organisations in which the chief information officer (CIO) is a member of the senior management team, is responsible for an integrated function that includes information security and already has the full trust and support of the CEO and the board. In such an organisation the CIO could be the driver of the project, but it will still need the CEO's commitment and support, not least so that everyone in the organisation understands that securing recognition is a business priority. The CIO will also urgently need to build a cross-business project team; I will return to this later.

The Project Mandate

The project mandate is where you capture initial evidence of this commitment in a usable format. A project mandate (or PID) is a document that is widely used to capture the key elements of any complex project. It ensures there is a single, original point of reference that sets out the three keys to project success: deliverables, timeline and budget.

Complex projects fail because one or more of these three project variables are poorly identified and/or managed. 'Scope creep' is one of the most common roots of project failure. Project mandates, therefore, seek to clearly identify project scope and to pin down the three variables in order to support an effective project governance process.

Your project mandate should address these four points:

1. Deliverables: identify the objective as the achievement of ISO 27001 certification for either a specific part or the whole of the organisation and, if possible, identify why information security is important for your organisation.
2. Timeline: create an outline project plan and target completion date on the basis of the nine steps to success.
3. Budget: identify the resources, both internal and external, as well as the training, software and tools that you are going to need for the project.
4. Authorisation to proceed: the mandate should contain management endorsement of the project and authorisation to proceed, to achieve the identified objectives using the budgeted resources.

Deliverables and the project objective

While the project deliverable is relatively easy to define (for example, achieve ISO 27001 certification within four months), you still need to be clear about the reasons for pursuing that objective as well as clarifying the difference between project objective and information security objectives.

The purpose of an information security management system is, of course, to reduce and control risks to your information. The actual objective (or objectives) of your ISMS project may be different to the purposes of the ISMS itself, and you should be clear about these differences if you are to appropriately focus both the project and the ISMS. The project objective may be, for instance, to secure ISO 27001 certification within a given time frame in order to meet a contractual or regulatory requirement, to improve business competitiveness or reduce the cost and complexity of sales and marketing responses to tender invitations. Project objectives, in other words, link specifically to business benefits that are to be derived from their achievement. Project objectives will usually be high-level and performance against them easy to track.

Information security objectives may be, but are not necessarily, related to the project objectives. Information security objectives will definitely be linked to the preservation of confidentiality, integrity and availability of information within the context of the organisation and in relation to its risk appetite. Progress toward achieving information security objectives must be measurable, which means the objectives themselves need to be specific, measurable, achievable, realistic and time-bound. Typical objectives might, for instance, be to reduce the number of disruptive information security incidents from 14 per year to two per year, or to increase network availability from

97% and 20×7×360 to 99.99999% and 24×7×365. Such objectives will be broken down into lower level objectives, with accountability for their achievement allocated to appropriate departments and levels within the organisation.

Gap analysis

Most organisations are already taking steps to manage their information security. While there may be significant vulnerabilities, it's not as though nothing is currently being done! The starting point for your project is usually, therefore, to understand how far your current practices are from the requirements set out in ISO 27001, and the best way to do this is with what we call a 'gap analysis'. This is a quick, reasonably high-level audit of your current information security management practices against the requirements set out in ISO 27001, which identifies where there is a shortfall and also identifies what resources and capabilities you have in place for closing the gap, or what resources you might need to bring from outside.

If you have already defined information security objectives, your gap analysis could also identify what steps still need to be taken in order to achieve those objectives.

You might call the output from the gap analysis a 'security improvement plan' or 'SIP'. This SIP becomes, in effect, your ISMS Project Plan.

Budget and resources

You can't implement an ISO 27001 ISMS on your own, or without some investment in tools and training. For ISO 27001, 'resources' means human, technical, information and financial resources. Purpose-designed tools are likely to reduce project time, error and cost. The two most useful tools are documentation templates and risk assessment software. The risk assessment solution we most recommend is available directly from Vigilant Software, here: *www.vigilantsoftware.co.uk*.

A number of people across the organisation, and from different levels within it, will need to contribute. You may also want to bring in external consultants, whether for guidance or because you need additional resource to execute your project plan.

There are a number of specialist areas in which consultants can be helpful:

- You can use consultants – trusted third parties – to communicate the seriousness of the information risks faced by the organisation and the need, therefore, for an ISMS.

- You can use consultants to provide advice on specific (most often technical) issues – for instance, scoping and how external or internal threats might affect your decisions about project scope – to carry out a risk assessment, to deal with documentation, or to advise on integration with other management systems.

- You can (and might be well-advised) to use consultants to help you identify appropriate technical controls for specific risks that you've identified. This holds true as long as the consultants have no financial interest in any solutions they might recommend and fully understand and can help you apply the two key financial measures of return on investment (ROI) and total cost of ownership (TCO) to any solutions they propose.

- You can use consultants in a mentoring capacity, to review critical documents and as a sounding board with whom you can discuss key steps in your project and key issues that you have to deal with, and possible solutions.

You do not need to hire external consultants in order to achieve ISO 27001. Many organisations get the job done completely under their own steam. Many other organisations simply don't have the time and resource to structure, manage and deliver an ISMS project without additional input. Whether or not you hire consultants is, therefore, a function of resource availability within your organisation, budget and your organisation's cultural preference for working things out for itself versus bringing in outside expertise.

The major benefits of using outside consultants should be that:

- even if they are only working on your project one day per week, their time with you is focused exclusively on your project, and
- they have significant ISO 27001 implementation experience, which should help you avoid blind alleys, over-detailed or impractical methodologies, disjointed implementations or losing the plot entirely.

If you use consultants, it should go without saying that they should be able to point at substantial experience implementing ISO 27001 and, of course, that they themselves are ISO 27001 certified.

The 'do-it-yourself' approach can be simplified and accelerated by using the kinds of established tools and techniques discussed in this book, and by following this nine-step methodology.

The output from your gap analysis is therefore an ideal starting point for determining the resource requirements of the project, starting with whether or not you intend to use external consultants or will be recruiting for key internal ISMS or project roles. It's particularly useful to identify who will be needed on the ISMS project team (we'll discuss this shortly); who will be invited to contribute from across the business; who will have the key project roles and responsibilities; who owns the project; who the project reports to internally; how progress is tracked and reported; etc.

The major benefit of identifying your resource requirements in your PID is that, once top management have signed off on the project, you should be able to rely on having access to those resources. In any organisation where a considerable part of the required resource will have other duties and responsibilities, this is a major benefit!

Those who are involved with the ISMS will need to be competent to carry out their roles. I'll return to the issue of competence later, but you will need to start taking steps to acquire competent personnel right away!

Apart from training and skill development, resource requirements may also include software, toolkits, staff awareness e-learning, training and/or consultancy support. Each of those options will be addressed at appropriate points in this book.

Timeline and outline project plan

Your gap analysis should also enable you to create an outline project plan, most sensibly in the form of a Gantt chart. At this stage, it can be quite high-level, setting out timelines, milestones and key objectives. The end point of your project plan should, of course, be the achievement of your project objective within the planned project timeframe; your information security objectives are likely to be pursued and achieved over much longer time frames.

As your project planning becomes more detailed, so will your Gantt chart; you will, however, still want to stay within the original timelines and will want to avoid disruptions to the project that could have an impact on the timeline you've committed to achieving.

Project Initiation Document

A PID is a formal document; most commonly used within a PRINCE2® project, the concept applies just as well to any complex project that involves multiple contributors, a number of whom may have multiple roles both inside and outside the project. It is also an excellent way to record the project objectives clearly and to have the key initial components of the project approved by top management.

If your organisation already has a process that meets these needs, you should use it: the sooner the ISMS project can be evidently set within your business as usual arrangements, the better. If you do not already have such a process, you can either create one yourself, or simply purchase the PID toolkit from one of our websites.

Within your document management system the PID should be treated as a record; after all, that's what it is!

CHAPTER 2: PROJECT INITIATION

The project mandate is the first step in getting your ISMS project off the ground. The second step is to set up the project itself and the project governance structure, effectively an extension of what is contained in the PID. The project governance structure needs to be more elaborate for complex, lengthy projects than for quick, relatively straightforward ones.

The project governance structure will consist of:

- The project objective;
- The project team, typically with a project board for projects that are scheduled to take longer than nine months;
- A project plan (who, when) that is a more detailed version of the high-level project plan included with the PID, including scheduled review dates;
- A project risk register.

Objectives

The project and information security objectives will feed into the information security policy and will start to inform the ISO 27001 requirements around monitoring, measurement, analysis and evaluation, and management review. It will include a time-bound statement regarding achievement of either certification or compliance to the Standard, as applicable, plus the definition of high-level information security objectives.

Project management

As part of putting together the PID, you should already have determined who the project owner will be and, if possible, who will chair the project team/working group. At this point, you would ideally start creating a RACI matrix for the project. This identifies who should be Responsible, Accountable, Consulted and Informed regarding key project decisions and each of the information security management processes as they're drawn up.

The project team should be made up of roles that have responsibility for representing the interests of every key part of the organisation; this does not mean that every part of the organisation must be directly represented, as that might create a huge and unwieldy team, but that each person on the team should be aware of whose interests they need to look out for. There should also be a spread of levels of seniority, with delegated authority from the respective manager(s).

Project leadership

Unless the CEO is personally leading the project, you should ask for the following active support:

- That the CEO makes a point of understanding the business benefits of pursuing an information security strategy, and the return on investment (more on this below) this project will achieve for the organisation.
- That the CEO leads a presentation (which you will prepare) on the information security strategy to the board, includes ISMS certification in the organisation's business goals for the year, secures board support for the objective expressed in the project mandate and arranges

for ongoing board monitoring of project progress throughout its life (which will ensure the project achieves and maintains the sort of political profile that will improve its chances of success).

- That the CEO personally leads presentations (which you will prepare) on the project to the executive or senior management of the organisation as well as to all the staff in each of the organisational forums that are used for staff communication.

- That the CEO nominates his/her most senior business line executive to support the project and lead the steering group (on which, more below), to provide day-to-day backing and support for you, and to lead the change management effort. This person has to be personally committed to the success of the project, prepared to do whatever is necessary to succeed.

- That the CEO clearly sets out – for senior management and for everyone in the organisation - the prioritisation for this project and your authority to seek the input and involvement of all whose contribution will be essential to your success.

- That the CEO sets a personal example of applying all the work practices and following all the procedures that will become part of the new ISMS.

Senior management support

Senior management support is equally important. An ISMS project cuts across all parts of the organisation and you therefore need to be sure that all key leaders are on side. Of course, there will always be varying degrees of enthusiasm for an ISMS project and not all of the senior management will be as enthusiastic as you would like them to be. There are two important steps in securing the support you will need from this group:

1. Set up a cross-organisational steering group to drive the project forward. This steering group should be led either by the CEO or by the CEO's nominated deputy and should be primarily a business-orientated group. In other words, it should consist primarily of business managers who have a direct personal interest in the effectiveness of any ISMS project and whose contribution will ensure that the ISMS meets business needs and becomes a fully functional part of the organisation. This group should include any individuals who are likely to resist the project and, if possible, they should be given key responsibilities leading to success of the project. If this is unlikely to work, alternative methods of isolating them should be pursued – this is one area in which a committed CEO should be asked to provide personal input.

   Finally, I can't stress how important it is for this group not to have a preponderance of IT or technical people enough – the project must be seen as a business project, not an IT one. This group might, depending on the size of the organisation, be the project group. In larger organisations, the steering group will be responsible for 'operationalising' the board approved plan for implementation of an ISMS, delegating detailed work to a project group and monitoring progress on a regular basis. Those who are members of the steering group should be barred from sending junior members of their teams in their place. Finally, bear in mind that steering groups should be small; three to seven people is the optimum range for effective oversight and decision-making.

2. The CEO should make the initial presentation to the steering group. This presentation should focus on the information security risks faced by the organisation and the potential impacts of a failure to implement proper security on the organisation, and should set out the relative prioritisation and importance that the project has. It should be clear to everyone in the steering group that this project carries the CEO's personal endorsement, and that it will receive high-level oversight throughout its life.

Project team

In large organisations, it might be appropriate to have the dual-level management structure described above, with a management steering group and an executive project team. The steering group would be responsible for strategy, project governance and ISMS oversight. The executive team would be responsible for designing, implementing and operating the ISMS. In smaller organisations, the functions of both groups are typically embedded in a single project group. Either or both of these groups might have the characteristics of what is often called a 'cross-functional forum'.

This project group, or team, should be drawn from those parts of the organisation most likely to be affected by the implementation of the ISMS, and there should also be a *very small* number of functional experts, including HR/personnel. The balance is important; a properly functioning ISMS depends on everyone in the business understanding and applying its controls and, if the project team is made up of a preponderance of non-technical people, it is more likely to produce something that everyone in the business understands. The team should certainly include at least one experienced project manager, who will be responsible for tracking and reporting progress against the planned objectives. The project team should report directly to either the chairman of the steering group or (preferably) the CEO and should have the appropriate delegated authority to implement the mandated ISMS project plan. Clauses 7.1 and 7.2 of ISO 27001 require, between them, the provision of adequate and competent resources to establish, maintain and continually improve the ISMS, and putting an appropriately structured project team in place is the first step in doing so.

Project team members should be selected from those in senior positions across the organisation. Key functions that should be represented are quality/process management, human resources, training and IT and facilities management, as they will all have to change their working practices significantly as a result of the decision to implement an ISMS. Apart from the manager responsible for information security and a trained information security expert, the most critical representation will be from sales, operations and administration. Obviously, non-sales organisations (public sector and non-profits, for instance) have units that work with stakeholders and these should also be involved. The functions in which the majority of the organisation's personnel are employed are the ones that will be most affected by the implementation of an ISMS. Ideally, the people invited to represent these functions should be among the most senior and widely respected individuals within them.

As mentioned earlier in this book, the change process that ISO 27001 implementation will require has a cultural impact. It is critical that those most able to represent and articulate the needs and concerns of the key parts of the organisation are included in the working party. Without their involvement, there is unlikely to be the buy-in necessary for the ISMS to be effectively developed and implemented.

Project team chair

The choice of chair for the project team is usually critical to its success, both as a group and in terms of how the rest of the organisation views and responds to it. The chair needs, therefore, to be someone who is capable of commanding the respect of all members of the project team. They need to be wholly committed to achieving the goal of a certified ISMS within the board-agreed timetable. They need to be pragmatic and prepared to 'think outside the box' in identifying solutions to organisational problems that are affecting implementation.

This person should not be from any one of the organisation's support functions as this will usually brand the project as an unimportant one. It should, on no account, be led by an IT person, as the implementation of an ISMS simply cannot afford to be seen as only an IT project. Preferably, they should have a broad managerial responsibility within the organisation as well as experience in implementing cross-organisational change projects. Ideally, they will be the chief executive or the main board director who has been charged with implementation of the board's security policy.

In smaller organisations, this person might also be the manager responsible for information security (described below); in larger organisations, where this is likely to be a full time role, the manager responsible for information security should properly report to the chair of the steering group or the CEO.

Not only is the structure outlined here the most effective method for delivery of the ISMS, it is also very clear evidence of commitment to its implementation from the very top of the organisation. The external ISO 27001 auditor will expect to see such evidence.

Information security manager

Whatever decision you make about the use of consultants, you will need to appoint an information security manager. It is good sense for one manager to be made responsible for all security related activities – both strategic and day-to-day – within the organisation. This person could be appointed before the steering group and/or project team is set up, and their brief could include the formation of the steering group and/or project team. The benefit of this route is speed and, potentially, simplicity. The board member who has been charged with the responsibility for ensuring implementation of the ISMS could simply select and appoint an appropriate person, who could then get on with putting together an appropriate project team, which could then take things forward. By contrast, the selection and training of the members of the steering group is potentially more time consuming and the period during which they are learning their roles will precede the point at which they are competent to select and appoint an appropriate manager. The organisation may not wish to pursue this slower route.

While the information security manager does not need to be the same person who is appointed as the organisation's information security expert (the skill sets required for the managerial role, particularly in a larger organisation, may be different from those required for the security expert's role), this person will still need adequate training in information security matters. Obviously, the person selected for the managerial role will need to be an effective manager, with well-developed communications and project management skills.

Experience suggests ISO 27001 projects work best when a single person is given the responsibility for ensuring that the organisation's ISMS meets the requirements of the standard, and for reporting to top management on the performance of the ISMS. While these roles could be held by two separate individuals, they could also both be held by the information security manager.

Specialist information security advice

Information security has a number of technical aspects and many technical considerations must be taken into account when designing and implementing an ISMS. This does not mean, as I have said before, that the project should be led by a technologist, or that it should have anything other than a complete business focus. The organisation does need to have available to it a source of specialist information security advice, who can provide detailed input of information security threats, on appropriate control configurations and on reliable monitoring and auditing processes when required. This role can be difficult to fill on a part-time basis – you want your specialist to have a working and detailed knowledge of your organisation – but not all organisations can afford a full-time resource. This leaves two alternatives, both of which involve substantial training: appoint someone from within the IT team to the role, and ensure they are adequately trained on the information security issues, or appoint someone from elsewhere – possibly, in a small organisation, the information security manager – and ensure they have adequate technical training and depth of know-how. The choice between the two options will be a pragmatic one, informed by the characters, attributes and personal circumstances of the potential candidates.

In larger organisations, of course, the recruitment and appointment of such an expert should be a priority. The one issue to which such a person is unlikely to have had adequate exposure is the information security management standard and, therefore, steps should be taken to provide this person with specific ISMS training such as that provided by an IBITGQ ATO (Accredited Training Organisation).

Functional specialists

There are a number of functional specialists who will need to be involved in the project and whose contributions will need to be effectively inspired and coordinated. These people include the leaders of the IT unit, the head of HR, the risk assessment or risk management experts within the organisation, the premises security people and both the finance and internal audit teams. It is worth seeking their early involvement by including them in the initial rounds of briefings on the need for an information security management system, eliciting their views as to risks and threats, and considering their likely critical contributions.

While you should involve them early on – because with them you will succeed, whereas without them you are almost certain to fail – you should keep in mind and make sure they fully understand that this is a business project, one that will be led by and reflect the needs of the business.

Project plan

For a long time, planning has been seen as an essential pre-cursor to project success. Of course, while it is necessary, it is not sufficient – a well-planned project can still fail for any one of a number or reasons. At the highest level, ISMS project planning means dealing successfully with all the issues identified in this book; each of the nine steps is also a critical component of a successful ISMS project plan. At a more practical level, planning is essential to ISO 27001 success. For the purposes of an ISMS implementation, 'planning' includes dealing with issues like the deployment of consultants, how the project will be managed, how different management systems will be integrated and the identification of key responsibilities and resource requirements throughout the project life-cycle.

Anyone tackling an ISO 27001 project should, once the organisation has decided to go ahead, obtain and read *IT Governance – An International Guide to Data Security and ISO27001/ISO27002*, Sixth Edition. The book is unique, and provides comprehensive and detailed advice on most of the issues that you will encounter in implementing an ISMS. The advice in this overview book is consistent with, and dovetails very directly into, the contents of *IT Governance – An International Guide to Data Security and ISO27001/ISO27002*.

Just as helpfully, ISO 27001 is designed for better alignment or integration with related management systems within the organisation (for example, ISO 9001 and ISO 14001).

It should also be noted that ISO 27001:2013 allows an implementation project to address the requirements of the standard in any order – it specifically says that the sequence of the clauses should not be taken as setting out implementation precedence. However, starting at the beginning is still a very practical approach!

Structured approach to implementation

A structured ISMS implementation plan should follow the nine steps described in this book. The elements below should all be addressed in the detailed implementation planning:

- Set up your implementation project and project mandate, select a continual improvement model and determine your approach to documentation, set up the management framework, define the internal and external context of the organisation, identify the requirements of any interested parties and, taking these issues into account, define the scope of the ISMS.

- Obtain top management commitment to the ISMS, define an information security policy, and allocate roles and responsibilities – including a role responsible for reporting on the performance of the ISMS.

- Define a systematic approach to risk assessment and the risk acceptance criteria.

- Carry out a risk assessment to identify, within the context of the policy and ISMS scope, the important information assets of the organisation and the risks to them. This is where you assess the risks.

- Identify and evaluate options for the treatment of these risks, selecting the control objectives and controls to be implemented where required.

- Prepare a Statement of Applicability and a Risk Treatment Plan.

- Implement the Risk Treatment Plan and planned controls.

- Provide appropriate training for affected staff, as well as staff awareness programs.

- Manage operations and resources in line with the ISMS.

- Implement procedures that enable prompt detection of, and response to, security incidents.

- Implement procedures for monitoring, reviewing, testing and audit.

- Implement procedures for reviewing the ISMS and the outcomes of testing and audits in light of a changing risk environment, new technology or other circumstances. Improvements to the ISMS should be identified, documented and implemented.

Phased approach

In large, complex organisations, it might be practical to seek multiple certifications, one for each discrete part of the organisation, on the basis that this minimises the project complexity and allows for a phased approach to implementation. Where it really is possible to adequately define a scope for a subsidiary part of the organisation (and we'll deal more fully with scope as part of the management framework later), such that its information security needs can be independently assessed, it may be possible to gain substantial experience in designing and implementing an ISMS plus a track record of success and the momentum that accompanies it; this may mean that a subsequent roll-out to the rest of the organisation can be carried through successfully and smoothly. These considerations apply to any large, complex project and the appropriate answer depends very much on individual organisational circumstances.

While there are significant benefits to this 'step-by-step' approach, they will all be lost if scoping attempts to create 'artificial' business units, as these will not be accepted by external certification auditors.

The project plan

Normal project planning tools should be deployed in creating and managing the ISMS project. The plan should reflect the high-level timeline contained in the project mandate, be prepared by the project team and, once it has been critically tested by the CEO and top management, approved by the board. This plan has to be capable of being understood by senior management and the board and should, therefore, be capable of appearing on two sides of A4. It should also provide sufficient scope for those who will have to implement the plan to find appropriate solutions to the many operational challenges that will turn up. It should not, in other words, be an overly-detailed plan – although the thinking behind it should be detailed.

A key preliminary step in any successful change programme is to identify and isolate, or convert, potential opposition. Where an ISMS roll out is concerned, there is sometimes internal resistance from within the IT department. There are a number of possible reasons for this, including the desire of the IT team not to lose control of IT security (particularly where ISO 27001 certification has been set as an IT department responsibility), the IT department's desire to maintain its mystique and the fear that its existing controls might be found to be inadequate.

This is not surprising. ISO 27001 does require the organisation's board and senior management to take control of its ISMS and the whole organisation to get behind and understand key aspects of security policy. The resistance of the IT department can sometimes be expected and must be overcome at the outset. There are circumstances where this can lead to a change in IT staff, either forced or unforced, and the organisation should expect this and prepare appropriate contingency plans.

Integration with existing security management systems

ISO 27001:2013 does not require a sequential approach to the establishment and implementation of an ISMS. In reality, once they realise the scale of the information risks they face, many organisations will want to tackle a number of the necessary tasks in parallel. Certainly, most organisations will come to ISO 27001 with some information security structures and controls already in place and with a question as to how to intelligently integrate these with any new ones.

Most organisations that embark on ISO 27001 already have a number of information security measures in place, usually to meet existing contractual, regulatory or business requirements. We call these the baseline controls; your ISMS project should ensure that those controls already in place are adequate and appropriate and that additional required controls are implemented as quickly as possible.

The Statement of Applicability will only be complete once all the identified risks have been assessed and the applicability of all the identified controls has been considered and documented. Usually, the Statement is started before any controls are implemented and completed as the final control is put in place.

Quality system integration

Many organisations that tackle ISO 27001 may already have an ISO 9001 certificated quality assurance system in place. ISO 27001 was written within the international ISO framework, which is designed to encourage integration of management systems within organisations. The ISMS should be integrated with the quality assurance system to the greatest extent possible. In particular, ISO 27001 Clause 7.5, which deals with documentation and document control records, can (and should) be met by applying any existing documentation control requirements of an existing ISO 9000 management system. Procedures and other documents within the ISMS have to be controlled. The logical decision for any organisation that implements an ISMS is to adopt the ISO 9000 approach.

Effectively, therefore, what one could be doing is *extending* an existing management system to include information security management, not bringing in a whole new system. This is an important message that should underpin the organisation's change management and communication plans; the smaller the perceived mountain, the more quickly an organisation will set out to climb it.

In circumstances where the organisation does not already have an existing ISO 9001 certified management system and wants guidance on the documentation, document control and records issues of ISO 27001, it should obtain and use the guidance in any current manual on the implementation of ISO 9001.

It is also important that the assessment and certification body chosen by the organisation understands and accepts this integrated approach. If it does not, get a new one; the task of having the existing system re-assessed (and only at the next planned surveillance date) is much smaller than the task of creating and implementing a wholly new and parallel ISMS.

Looking ahead

The project team will have to put in place a communications strategy dealing with both internal and external audiences – potentially including stakeholders and shareholders, partners, regulatory bodies, customers, suppliers, etc. – and a staff awareness policy, as well as identifying what competencies and skills the organisation will need in order to address its information security objectives. These two items, to which I will return in due course, should be on the project agenda from early on.

Costs and project monitoring

The PID contains the approved project budget and high-level project plan. It is the responsibility of project managers to collate and review data about progress and budget utilisation, as well as the effectiveness of project risk management measures; the board (or, in a dual-level project structure, the steering group) should review this information on a regular basis, as part of its regular business project review.

The review dates mandated by the board can evolve over time into ISMS review dates, at which point frequency might shift from monthly to annually.

The key points to perform a project progress review are:

- After planned completion of each of the nine steps.

- After completion of the draft Statement of Applicability (SoA). Any costs incurred prior to this should be minimal but, until the SoA defines what needs to be done, it will not be possible to budget effectively for the implementation.

- After implementation of the initial suite of procedures that put in place the management framework (discussed later in this book).

- After completion of the first cycle of system audits and reviews and prior to the initial visit by the certification body.

- Annually, as part of the regular review of the ISMS, to ensure that the budget is being correctly applied and that any new technology issues, risk, threats or vulnerabilities have been identified and taken care of.

Risk register

The project team should, at commencement of the project, identify the risks to the success of the project. While these typically arise from internal issues – such as a traditionally open and insecure culture, inadequate management commitment, inadequate project or information security resources, competing demand for resource time and effort, etc. – they may also be triggered by external issues, such as upcoming changes to data protection regulations or security demands triggered by specific clients.

These risks should be listed in the project risk register. Each risk should have an owner, and there should be a plan to mitigate each of the risks by reducing likelihood and/or impact. The project team should review its identified risks, and the effectiveness of its risk management plans, on a regular basis; this key process can make a substantial difference to the effective implementation of the ISMS project plan.

CHAPTER 3: ISMS INITIATION

The first concrete steps in initiating the ISMS are to determine which continual improvement methodology to use and to put a document structure in place.

Continual improvement

ISO 27001 recognises that a 'process approach' is the most effective method for managing information security. The Standard is open to the deployment of any continual improvement approach and allows for organisations that already use, for instance, the ITIL® 7 Step Continual Service Improvement approach, the COBIT® Continual Improvement Life Cycle or any other approach that may be appropriate in the organisation's context, to be certified. One of the most widely known and widely used approaches in the management system world is the 'Plan-Do-Check-Act' (PDCA) model, which will be familiar to quality and business managers everywhere.

Whichever continual improvement model is selected, it should be understood before work starts and should inform every step. It should have the idea of 'root cause analysis' (RCA) built or added into it; RCA contributes to identifying whether or not similar issues exist, or could potentially exist, elsewhere in the ISMS and this will enhance the effectiveness of the process – not only for nonconformities (as required by the Standard), but for all issues requiring correction and corrective action.

A common root cause analysis technique is the '5 Whys'. This is a technique for determining the root cause of a problem or defect by repeating the question 'Why?' five times. Each question forms the basis of the next question. While a sixth or seventh iteration might sometimes be necessary, the objective of the technique is to ensure that assumptions are questioned and that the real root cause of a problem is identified so that it can be addressed.

Security improvement plan

I earlier identified that the ISO 27001 project could be tackled as a security improvement plan, using a gap analysis as the starting point. Clearly, if this is the way you're going, you need to determine your continual improvement methodology early and ensure that you report progress through your continual improvement log.

Expanding the RACI matrix

At this stage, you would also expand the RACI matrix by identifying who is initially to be formally accountable for the most important roles in the ISMS.

The roles that need to be identified are the owners of:

- Oversight of the establishment, implementation, operation, maintenance, and improvement of the ISMS;
- Continual improvement;
- Information security risk assessment; and
- Managing information security incidents.

Documentation

Your risk assessment process determines the controls that have to be deployed in your ISMS, and your Statement of

Applicability identifies the controls that you are deploying in the light of your approach to risk management. Every one of those controls, together with your approach to identifying and managing risk, your management structure, your decision-making processes and every other component of your ISMS has to be documented; as a point of reference; as the basis for ensuring that there is consistent application over time; and to enable continual improvement.

Documentation will be the most time consuming part of the total project and, therefore, how you decide to tackle this aspect will be a major determinant of your overall success. Documentation has to be complete, comprehensive, in line with the requirements of the Standard and fit your organisation like a glove. A properly managed ISMS will be fully documented. ISO 27001 describes the minimum documentation that should be included in the ISMS, i.e. what is needed to meet the Standard's requirement that the organisation maintain sufficient records to demonstrate compliance.

The key test of the ISMS documentation is that it should be adequate, but not excessive, and that it enables each of the processes to be "systematically communicated, understood, executed and effective so as to be repeatable and dependable".

The documents include:

- The information security policy, the scope statement for the ISMS, the risk assessment, the various control objectives, the Statement of Applicability and the Risk Treatment Plan. The scope of the ISMS (the minutes of board and steering committee meetings endorsing this can also be helpful).

- The management framework documentation (see the next chapter).

- The underpinning, documented procedures (which should include responsibilities and required actions) that implement specific controls. A procedure describes who has to do what, under what conditions, or by when. These procedures (there would probably be one for each of the implemented controls) would be part of the policy manual which, itself, can be on paper or electronic.

- Documents that deal with how the ISMS is monitored, reviewed and continually improved, including measuring progress toward the information security objectives.

All formal documentation should be controlled and available to all staff who are entitled to view it. It can be published in paper form but is most effective on an intranet, a shared drive or SharePoint. A shared drive or SharePoint ensures that the current version of any procedure is immediately available to all members of staff without hassle. A structured numbering system should be adopted that ensures ease of navigation of the documentation, that document issue is controlled, that replacement pages and changes are tracked and that the documentation is complete. Staff should be trained in how to use the documentation and how to draft operations procedures for the assets and processes for which they are personally responsible.

Clearly, there will be a number of security system documents that need to be subject to security measures. These will include documents such as the risk assessment, the Risk Treatment Plan and the Statement of Applicability, which contain important insights into how security is managed and should therefore be classified, restricted and treated in accordance with the organisation's information classification system. Access should be limited to people with specified ISMS roles, such as the information security adviser.

Four levels of documentation

ISO 27001 clearly recognises that there is no such thing as a 'one size fits all' approach to documentation. Instead, it recommends that the extent of the ISMS documentation should reflect the complexity of the organisation and its security requirements. In practical terms, there are four levels of documentation in an ISMS, and each level has different characteristics, including about who is entitled to make decisions regarding revisions to the documents. The four levels are:

1. The board-approved corporate policy, which drives all other aspects of the ISMS. This high-level policy is supported by a number of additional, subject-specific policies (setting out, for instance, what constitutes acceptable use of the internet).

2. Detailed procedures, that describe who is responsible for doing what, when and in what order.

3. Operations/work instructions, that set out in detail precisely how each of the identified tasks are performed.

4. Records, which provide evidence as to what was done.

The amount of work increases as you descend the four levels, once, of course, those have been brought into line with the control requirements; the most demanding, in terms of time, is producing the third level – even though this is essentially the documentation of existing ways of carrying out specific activities.

Documentation approaches

There are three approaches to tackling the documentation requirements of the Standard, two traditional and one using a documentation toolkit. In an organisation that meets the criteria described earlier in this book, the length of time that the project will require will depend very much on the methodology adopted.

Trial and error

The first is a methodology known as 'trial and error' and, because those charged with deploying the ISMS first have to learn how to perform every single aspect of the task, it is the most time-consuming of the three, has a high risk of failure and extends the period during which the organisation continues failing to meet its information security objectives.

External expertise

The second, equally traditional, method is to bring in outside expertise in the form of experienced consultants to produce your documentation. It is a quicker approach than trial and error, but substantially more expensive. Its major advantages include considerably reducing project time, reducing the risk of failure, increasing the speed of organisational learning and overcoming resource deficiencies.

Third party documentation toolkit plus guidance

While this approach is most appropriate for organisations that prefer to tackle internal change projects largely without external consultant support, it is an approach that depends for its success as much on the quality and extent of senior management support and commitment as it does on the quality of the tools themselves.

The major advantages of this approach are that documentation toolkits:

- are fit for purpose – designed to meet ISO 27001 requirements from the outset;

- are fast to deploy;

- are very cost-effective (with low TCO and high ROI);

- generate substantial cost savings in comparison to traditional approaches;

- are full of best practice;

- will be cross-functional, company-wide, with a correct continual improvement cycle;

- create a very low likelihood of project failure;

- have continuous improvement built in from the start.

It is essential that any documentation toolkit be designed to meet the detailed requirements of the Standard, and that it comes with detailed guidance on how to tackle the project and all of the detailed drafting requirements. At IT Governance, we designed and built a documentation toolkit that exactly meets the requirements of the Standard, reflects multiple successful deployments of certifiable information security management systems and that was developed specifically for organisations that want to avoid the costs and disadvantages of learning by trial and error. These toolkits are also specifically designed so that they can easily be integrated into additional management systems, ensuring that the opportunity to build an integrated management system that meets multiple standards is available from the outset.

There is a free, trial version of this toolkit available for download through each of our websites. It is worth taking a look at this toolkit as part of your preparatory research into how you are going to tackle the documentation part of your project.

Third party documentation

As part of the documentation processes, one should also be introduced for control of documents of external origin, including their retention periods.

CHAPTER 4: MANAGEMENT FRAMEWORK

ISO 27001 is a specification for an information security *management* system. Unsurprisingly, therefore, it sets out requirements for a management framework. The fourth step in the ISMS implementation is to create this management framework.

Clause 4 of ISO 27001 says the organisation must identify the needs and expectations of interested parties, as well as the internal context of the organisation, and that these should be taken into account in establishing the scope of the ISMS.

You started to identify these requirements when creating your project risk register, so you should revisit this information and build on it. The external context will include the business and risk environment, what's going on in your sector, and any other developments that might impact your information security stance. The internal context is the range of internal issues that will affect how you design and deploy the management system; the Standard is saying, in effect, that your ISMS must be designed for your business.

As part of this internal context, you will want to begin identifying the organisation's risk appetite; this will be a significant issue in many aspects of implementation and I will return to it later in this book.

The requirements of interested parties are more complex. Interested parties can include regulators, partners and customers. The Payment Card Industry Data Security Standard (PCI DSS), for instance, is a commercial requirement imposed by an acquiring bank; data protection activities are imposed by law and policed by regulators. All organisations are faced with a multitude of such compliance requirements, each of which imposes a specific set of information security controls and brings important variations in requirements for preserving confidentiality, integrity and availability.

The IT Governance Compliance Database is a tool that was designed to make available, to UK organisations, the complete set of approximately 100 relevant laws and regulations, identifying the specific clauses that impose compliance requirements and allowing for the addition of multiple third party contracts that bring their own specific needs.

All these compliance requirements will need to feed into your ISMS, into your risk assessment and into your risk treatment documentation. Although the Standard does not require it, it is worth documenting all these aspects for ease of reference and of review in future.

As part of documenting the organisation's context, it would make sense to review and (re)confirm the information security objectives that were initially documented in the PID and then further developed when initiating the project.

Scoping

Scoping is fundamentally important. Your management system scope will be stated on your compliance certificate. It will inform the audit as well as the external parties who are interested in your ISMS. It is key, both because you need to know the boundaries of what you are planning to implement, and because the Standard itself requires it.

One way of thinking about scoping is from the perspective of your information security policy.

Clause 5.2 of ISO 27001 sets out the requirements in respect of the ISMS policy clearly. The policy must be approved by the board. The policy must provide an overall sense of information security direction for the organisation as well as including information security objectives. It must include meeting information security requirements (which might be business, contractual or regulatory in nature) and it must also contain a commitment to continually improve the ISMS.

The ISMS policy applies across all parts of the organisation that are within the scope of the ISMS. As I've said, the scope must take into account the characteristics of the business, its organisation, location, assets and technology – what the Standard calls the "external and internal context" of the organisation. ISO 27001 refers, at this point, to ISO 31000, the international best practice Standard for organisational risk management. For those organisations seeking to properly integrate risk management across all aspects of the business, this ISO 31000 link will be important.

Your policy requirements should drive your approach to scoping the ISMS and the project. Scope determination is harder for larger, complex organisations than it is for smaller ones. Scoping is essential though for any size of organisation: you have to decide which information assets you're going to protect and which ones you're not before you can decide on appropriate protection.

This should be a quick decision for a small or medium-sized business: the whole organisation. That's because there will probably be hard-wired connections between all the information systems and day-to-day working relationships within the business that make it either extremely difficult or impractical to try and segregate one part of the business from another. The notion of segregation is at the heart of effective scoping: ultimately, you are going to try and create an impregnable barrier between the part of your business that is within the scope of your project and everything else. You have to be categorical about what is inside your information fortress and what is outside, and this means that you don't want *any* information systems, devices or business units that are both inside *and* outside – because that will be your weakest link.

ISO 27001 explicitly requires you to consider "interfaces and dependencies between activities performed by the organisation, and those that are performed by other organisations"; in other words, you must identify what is outside the scope of your ISMS, be prepared to justify its exclusion and manage the associated risks appropriately. This is to help you ensure that you don't try to draw the boundaries too narrowly.

Endpoint security

In today's business environment, your defensive barrier has to operate at the individual device level and is highly dependent on user compliance with business procedures. In other words, your scoping decision needs to include all the information devices that people use in their jobs – such as Smartphones, wireless laptops, home offices, etc. – as well as the more obvious central office systems such as accounting, payment processing, production, sales and order management, email, office automation, etc.

There may well also be cloud-based components that have to be taken into account.

In larger, more complex businesses, you will also want to ensure the entity that is within scope has a clearly defined legal and management structure and that there is alignment with the compliance requirements – part of the reason for your information security system is to ensure that you are compliant with the myriad of laws and regulations, so it makes sense for the entity that has those compliance obligations to be fully within the scope of your information security project.

In other words, those parts of the organisation to which your ISMS is going to apply need to be clearly identified. You should bear in mind that an ISMS is a management system, a formal structure that management deploys to ensure that its policy in information security is applied consistently throughout an organisation for which that management is accountable. Scoping of the ISMS may therefore be done on the basis of corporate, divisional or management structure, or on the basis of geographic location.

A virtual organisation, or a dispersed, multi-site operation, may have different security issues than one located on a single site. In practical terms, a security policy and ISMS that encompasses all of the activities within a specific entity for which a specific board of directors or management team is responsible is more easily implemented than one that is to be applied to only part of the entity.

It is important to ensure the board of directors that is implementing the policy does actually have adequate control over the organisation specified within the scope of the information security policy it will be expected to approve, and that it will be able to give a clear mandate to its management team to implement it within that entity. In other words, it is essential to decide the boundary within which protection is to be provided and ensure the team involved has the power to provide it.

Defining boundaries

The business environment and Internet are each so huge and diverse that it is necessary to draw a boundary between what is within the organisation and what is outside. In simple terms, boundaries are physically or logically identifiable. Boundaries have to be identified in terms of the organisation, or part of the organisation, that is to be protected, which networks and which data, and at which geographic locations.

The organisation that is within the scope must be capable of physical and/or logical separation from third parties and from other organisations within a larger group. While this does not exclude third party contractors, it does make it practically very difficult (though not necessarily impossible) to put an ISMS in place within an undifferentiated organisation that shares significant network and/or information assets or geographic locations. A division of a larger organisation that, for instance, shares a group head office and head office functions with other divisions, could not practically implement a meaningful ISMS. Usually, the smallest organisational entity that is capable of implementing an ISMS is one that is self-contained. It will have its own board of directors or management team, its own functional support, its own premises and its own IT network, or will have IT services supplied to it by a group or other supplier, subject to some form of service level agreement.

It is not unusual for divisions of larger organisations to independently pursue certification; the critical factor is the extent to which they can practically differentiate themselves and their business and information systems from other divisions of the same parent organisation.

For larger – usually highly decentralised – organisations that have a multiplicity of systems and cultures and an extensive geographic spread, it is often simpler as a general rule to tackle ISO 27001 and risk assessment on the basis of smaller business units that meet the general description set out above. Larger – more centralised – organisations that have a single business culture and largely common business and information systems throughout are probably better off creating a single ISMS.

It is critical, if there are aspects of the organisation's activities or systems that are to be excluded from the requirements of the security policy, that these are clearly identified – and explained – at the scoping stage. Multi-site or virtual organisations will need to carefully consider the different security requirements of their different sites and the management implications of them. There should be clear boundaries ("defined in terms of the characteristics of the organisation, its location, assets and technology") within which the security policy and ISMS will apply. Any exclusions should be openly debated by the board and the steering group, and the minutes should set out how and why the final scoping decision was taken.

It is possible that, in fact, divisions of the organisation, components of the information system or specific assets will not be able to be excluded from the scope either because they are already so integral to it or because their exclusion might have the effect of undermining the information security objectives themselves. It must, therefore, be clear that any exclusions do not in any way undermine the security of the organisation that is implementing the ISMS.

For an ISMS certification, auditors are required to assess how management applies its information security policy across the whole of the organisation that is defined as being within the scope of the policy. You should expect them to test the boundaries of the stated scope to their limits to ensure that all interdependencies and points of weakness have been identified and adequately dealt with.

In reality, as stated earlier, the process of designing and implementing an effective ISMS may be made simpler by including the entire organisation for which the board has responsibility.

Network mapping

It can help (but is not essential) to make a network map that shows how your central management and information systems link together and which identifies all of the points at which the outside world can interact with your network. This map will be very simple for a small organisation (because the network is simple) and far more complex for a larger, more complex organisation. The initial map that you draw to aid your initial scoping exercise will need to be extended as part of the detailed project planning phase to ensure that all aspects of your information systems have been identified. You do not need a detailed initial map; you just need to know how you will get from the initial one to the detailed one.

There is a range of network mapping software that will automatically map your network for you, some of which has additional helpful management features. The benefit of using such a tool is that it will quickly, completely and competently identify how your network is structured, what types of services are running and what access points and devices there actually are – and a status report of what is actually happening is much more useful than relying on a theoretical map.

Network maps are often drawn using software tools such as SmartDraw and Microsoft Visio, although you can start with a whiteboard and hand-draw a network diagram before attempting to model it with a software tool. Your network map will ultimately need to identify in detail all the devices (e.g. workstations 43, servers 6) that are connected to it, as well as their functions (e.g. print and file server, domain controller, etc.).

Cutting corners

All our experience teaches that it is a mistake to define the scope too narrowly. By 'too narrowly', I mean a scope that, for instance, includes only a head office, or only that bit of the organisation that is under pressure from third party (usually government) funders or customers to become certified. While it may appear, on the surface, that this is a route to a quick and easy certification, it is often in fact a route to a worthless certificate.

In the long run any external party assessing the nature of an organisation's ISMS will want to be sure that all the critical functions that may affect its relationship are included, and a limited scope will not do this. We are aware that some certification organisations are prepared to consider scopes that cover less than a complete business unit and, in our opinion, they are doing a disservice to their clients as well as to the integrity of the ISO 27001 schemes. Do not be tempted to use such certification bodies.

In conclusion, I recognise that scoping the ISMS can be very difficult in large, complex organisations. It is certainly an area where experienced, professional support can be helpful in assessing the best way forward, although I would recommend only using consultants who adopt much of the approach set out in this chapter. This is important because the wrong scoping decision can, in the long run, invalidate the certificate you do achieve, leave key parts of your organisation open to all the risks that you are attempting to exclude and, when you finally focus on the need to do the job properly, will be far more expensive than if you'd done it right in the first place. Worse, because you did it wrong in the first place, it will be far harder to get adequate commitment and support for an extended project across the organisation than it would have been if you'd sold the whole project to the organisation in the first place.

Formalise key arrangements

At this point, you should formalise:

- How you will demonstrate leadership and commitment (all the requirements of Clause 5.1 in the Standard, building on the project mandate).

- The final version of the information security policy.

- The first full version of the RACI matrix, setting out organisational roles, responsibilities and authorities.

- The communication policy that identifies who is to communicate with which audiences, when and through which means. The communications process should include a method to ensure the message(s) in question has been correctly received and understood.

- The competence requirements for the generic ISMS roles, such as top management, risk owner, internal auditor, etc., as well as those identified when initiating the project and the ISMS. Bear in mind that you will also need competent individuals who can implement and maintain the selected information security controls, plus people who can deal with IT security, physical security and legal compliance. At least one member of the project team, ideally the project manager, should be required to have something like the IBITGQ CIS LI certificate.

- You should ensure that you have adequate resources to achieve the ISMS objectives.

Information security policy

The information security policy is the main driving force for the ISMS; it sets out the board's policy on, and requirements in respect of, information security. It should be a short document, but it has to capture board requirements and organisational reality while meeting the requirements of the Standard. There is a full discussion of the issues involved in, and development process required for, an information security policy statement in *IT Governance – An International Guide to Data Security and ISO27001/ISO27002, Sixth Edition.*

The board and management have to be completely behind and committed to the ISMS; therefore, the policy statement must be issued under their authority and there should be clear evidence, in the form of written board minutes, that the policy was debated and agreed by the board as a whole and/or by the management steering group. Any revisions to the policy should also be agreed through the same route.

It will also require participation by all employees in the organisation and may require participation from customers, suppliers, shareholders and other third parties. This is part of the context of the ISMS referred to earlier. In thinking through the security policy, the board and the forum will need to consider how it will impact on these constituents and/or audiences and the benefits and disadvantages that the business will experience as a result of this. It is a good idea to start thinking these issues through before you commence the detailed process of designing and deploying your ISMS.

Communication strategy

Communication is important to ISO 27001 project success. Underlying every successful change management programme, and especially necessary for the successful roll out of an ISMS, is a well-designed and effectively implemented internal communications plan. Compliance with ISO 27001 and common sense both suggest that key components of this plan must include:

- Top down communication of the information security vision – why the ISMS is necessary, what the organisation's legal responsibilities are, what the business will look like when the programme is complete and what benefits it will bring to everyone in the organisation.

- Regular cascade briefings to all staff on progress against implementation plan objectives. These briefings should quickly become part of the existing organisational briefing cycle so that ISMS progress becomes part of the normal business process – 'just another thing that we're doing'.

- A mechanism for ensuring that key constituencies and individuals within the business are consulted and involved in the development of key components of the system. This ensures that they buy into the outcome and to its implementation, and is a key reason for structuring the steering group and project team as was suggested in chapter two.

- A mechanism for ensuring regular and immediate feedback from people in the organisation – or in affected third party organisations – so that their direct experience of the initial system as it is implemented can be used in the evolution of the final version. This can form part of your continuous improvement process and, more immediately, offer evidence of effective 'checking'.

- These face-to-face communications should be underpinned with an effective information sharing system. Usually this will be part of the corporate intranet, on which regular progress reports as well as detailed information on specific aspects of the ISMS, are posted. Email alerts can tell staff to access the intranet for new information whenever it is posted and the site can encourage feedback by means of a 'write to the CEO' function.

Of course, if the organisation doesn't currently have a well-developed internal communication process, it will need to develop one. Allowance should be made in the outline project planning timetable and resource allocation for the development of such a system. Do not try and take an ISMS project forward without an adequate internal communication process: information security controls depend to a very large extent on the informed and committed behaviour of individuals within the organisation and, as a result, you simply have to ensure that you can deliver this.

Staff buy-in

The initial staff briefing, the one that accompanies the project kick- off, should set out clearly the nature of the threats faced by the organisation and the possible costs, in both financial and non-financial terms, of information security breaches. *The Case for ISO27001:2013* and the chapters on information security risk and governance in *IT Governance – An International Guide to Data Security and ISO27001/ISO27002, Sixth Edition*, provide useful information that can underpin a communications strategy.

Wherever possible, local and/or industry specific information should additionally be sought and used in staff presentations as this gives immediacy and currency to the possible threats. Illustrations of the possible direct consequences to your own organisation should be developed in order to add make the situation more relatable and help all those involved to fully appreciate the need for the ISMS.

A key part of getting effective user buy-in is translating information security risks and technology issues into widely and clearly understood *business* ones. Boards and managements understand issues in terms of their impact on the business and, unless those impacts are clearly delineated, clearly credible and clearly quantified, they're not going to pay them much attention. The same is true of functional and business leaders across the organisation whose interest is, if anything, more parochially focused on their own specific issues. The truth is that they are less interested in the long term strategic needs of the organisation than they are in achieving the specific sets of goals that drive their own compensation or promotion possibilities.

All this means that you not only need to translate the information security imperatives into a small number of credible, quantified and relevant numbers for the board and senior management, you also need to make the ISMS initiative directly relevant to every single person on whose support you're going to rely. Like all organisational politics, there's almost certainly no single message that will do this job for everyone. You're going to need a single, strong organisation-wide, top-down commitment supported by a large number of one-on-one, locally focused discussions in which you set out how the ISMS project will specifically improve the business circumstances for each person to whom you talk.

A large part of effective project management is sales skills and a detailed understanding of the organisational politics; this is why it can be very hard for an outsider to succeed as project manager in delivering an ISMS project.

CHAPTER 5: BASELINE SECURITY CRITERIA

Step five is a straightforward one; it looks at the information security controls that you already have in place, assesses them for adequacy and incorporates them into your ISMS.

As I've said earlier, most organisations will have made a number of decisions about risks before even starting the ISO 27001 project (they have, after all, been in business for a time, dealing with threats and vulnerabilities for real) and will also have implemented a number of controls in order to comply with statutory, regulatory or contractual requirements. The organisation has to decide how it incorporates these existing controls into its ISMS and its risk assessment methodology.

The requirement is to implement controls that are appropriate for the organisation, its information security objectives and the identified business, legal, regulatory and contractual requirements. We call these requirements the baseline security criteria, because they create the criteria that determine the information security controls you have to put in place, irrespective of your risk appetite or risk assessment.

Your risk assessment methodology should therefore state clearly that the requirements of interested parties have led the organisation to implement specific controls which are called the baseline security controls, and that these controls are incorporated into the ISMS.

At this point, you should assess whether or not your existing baseline security controls are adequate to meet your compliance requirements. This is best tackled by using a comprehensive tool like the ISMS Compliance Database (which contains a comprehensive and detailed collection of all the potentially applicable UK legislation) to determine whether or not additional controls are necessary in order to meet all your obligations.

This is also a good time to make an inventory of your customer and partner contracts, to identify any specific information security controls contained therein, and to ensure that those controls are implemented within the business.

PCI DSS, Cyber Essentials, HIPAA and DPA compliance are all examples of formal requirements for the implementation of baseline security controls.

You also have to determine how you handle all the other controls that are already in place, the ones that you adopted at some earlier point to meet specific security criteria at the time. You either review them now for adequacy and effectiveness, or you recognise their existence and simply accept them as part of your baseline security control set, focusing your risk assessment on those remaining risks that are not yet appropriately treated. For example, a door is a control but, in assessing the security of a room you recognise that the door is already in place and either consider its adequacy as a control or accept it and focus on other entry routes ('attack vectors').

CHAPTER 6: RISK MANAGEMENT

Risk assessment is at the heart of the ISMS. Understanding its significance to the overall process is critical, and is one of the keys to project success. The board adopts an information security policy because there are a number of significant risks to the availability, confidentiality and integrity of the organisation's information, and it mandates the design and deployment of an ISMS in order to ensure that its policy is systematically and comprehensively implemented. The policy must, therefore, reflect the board's assessment of information security risks and opportunities. This doesn't mean the board needs to carry out a detailed risk assessment itself, but it does need to set out a clear, overall approach to risk that can be used to take forward the ISMS project.

The organisation needs, in other words, to determine its criteria for accepting risks and identify the levels of risk it will accept. It is a truism to point out that there is a relationship between the levels of risk and reward in any business. Most businesses, particularly those subject to formal corporate governance requirements, will want to be very clear about which risks they will accept and which they won't, the extent to which they will accept risks and how they wish to control them. Management needs to specify its approach, in general and in particular, so that the business can be managed within that context.

Information risk is one of a number of risks that the organisation must control and it should, to the greatest extent possible, apply a common risk management framework to all the risks with which it is faced.

The starting point for any ISMS project manager's consideration of risk is to embrace the existing risk management function (if there is one) inside the organisation in order to understand a) its overall approach to risk and b) its specific approach to information security risk. If the organisation doesn't have any such formal function, it is imperative that the current approach to identifying, assessing and controlling risk, and those involved in the activity, are identified as quickly as possible. You will need to ensure that there is a consistent, organisation-wide approach to managing the information security risks.

Introduction to risk management

All organisations face risks of one sort or another on a daily basis. Risk management is a discipline for dealing with non-speculative risks, those risks from which *only* a loss can occur. Speculative risks, on the other hand, those from which either a profit *or* a loss can occur, are the subject of the organisation's business strategy whereas non-speculative risks, those risks that can reduce the value of the assets with which the organisation undertakes its speculative activity, are (usually) the subject of a risk management plan. These are sometimes called permanent and 'pure' risks, in order to differentiate them from the crisis and speculative types. Usually, the identification of a risk as either speculative or permanent reflects the organisation's *risk appetite*.

Risk management plans have four, linked, objectives, which are to:

1. Eliminate risks;
2. Reduce those risks that can't be eliminated to 'acceptable' levels; and then to either

3. Live with them, exercising carefully the controls that keep them 'acceptable'; or

4. Transfer them, by means of insurance, to some other organisation.

Pure, permanent risks are usually identifiable in economic terms; they have a financially measurable potential impact upon the assets of the organisation. Therefore risk management strategies are usually based on an assessment of the economic benefits that the organisation can derive from an investment in a particular control; in other words, for every control that the organisation might implement, the calculation is that the cost of implementation should be outweighed by the economic benefits that derive from – or economic losses that are avoided as – a result of its implementation.

The organisation should define its criteria for accepting risks (for example, it might say that it will accept any risk the economic impact of which is less than the cost of controlling it) and for controlling risks (for example, it might say that any risk that has both a high likelihood and a high impact must be controlled to an identified level, or threshold).

This chapter only provides a brief introduction to, and overview of risk management. There is more detailed guidance on this process in *Information Security Risk Management for ISO27001/ISO27002*.

The ISO 27001 requirement is that the risk assessment should take into account both the organisation's context (internal and external) as well as the requirements of third parties that might be relevant to, or have an interest in, the organisation's approach to information security. In other words, the risk assessment must be *business-driven* and must reflect legal, regulatory and contractual requirements. This is one of the most important ideas in information security: we recommend the business, managed by its board of directors, should identify the threats to assets, vulnerabilities and impacts on the organisation and should determine the degree of risk that it is prepared to accept in the light of its business model, business strategy and investment criteria.

Baseline security controls

Step five in the ISMS implementation process is to identify and implement the controls that are required to meet the organisation's legal, regulatory and contractual obligations (and there might be a number of different obligations, depending on jurisdictions within which it operates). It is also necessary to identify any controls that might be required by customers and suppliers, or other contractual mandates, and to include them in the baseline control set. The ISMS Compliance Database (*www.itgovernance.co.uk/shop/p-715.aspx*) is a useful tool; it helps identify specific controls that might be required to control risks arising from a failure to meet legal, regulatory or contractual obligations.

Risk assessment

Risk assessment is defined in ISO 27000 as a process that combines risk identification, risk analysis and risk evaluation. Risk identification is the "process of finding, recognising and describing risks", risk analysis is the "systematic use of information to estimate risk" and risk evaluation is the "process of comparing the estimated risk against given risk criteria" to determine its significance.

In simpler terms, risk assessment is the systematic and methodical consideration of: a) the realistic likelihood of a risk occurring and b) the business harm likely to result from any such risks.

The risk assessment should be a formal process. In other words, the process should be planned and the input data, its analysis and the results should all be recorded. 'Formal' does not mean that technical risk assessment tools must be used although, in more complex situations, they are likely to improve the process and add significant value. The complexity of the risk assessment will depend on the complexity of the organisation and of the risks under review. The techniques employed to carry it out should be consistent with this complexity and the level of assurance required by the board.

Five-step risk assessment process

There are five steps to a successful risk assessment.

1. Establish a risk assessment framework
2. Identify risks
3. Analyse risks
4. Evaluate risks
5. Select risk management options

Experienced information security and risk management practitioners know that manual risk assessment methods are highly dependent on one or two individuals within the organisation, are time-consuming (trial and error) and costly to create, and often suffer from data and process inconsistencies that undermine the integrity and dependability of the results. They will therefore always use a purpose-built ISO 27001 risk assessment software tool – one that follows the five steps to successful risk assessment outlined above – in order to achieve their organisation's risk management objectives consistently and cost-effectively.

Who conducts the risk assessment?

Unless the organisation already has a risk management function staffed by people with training that enables them to carry out risk assessments, it will (depending on the complexity of the organisation) need to delegate the responsibility to a lead risk assessor. There are two ways of doing this. The first is to hire an external consultant (or firm of consultants) to do it. The second is to train someone internally. The second is preferable in most cases, as the risk assessment will need to be reviewed when circumstances change, and having the expertise in-house enables this to be done cost-effectively. If the organisation already has a trained information security adviser, this person could take on the role.

In circumstances where the organisation has existing arrangements with external suppliers for risk assessment services, or is in the process of setting up a risk management function or capability (in the context of responding to the requirements of the Turnbull Guidance, or Basel III, perhaps), then it should ensure from the outset that its information security risk assessment process is included.

Risk analysis

Qualitative risk analysis is by far the most widely used approach. Risk analysis is a subjective exercise in any environment where returns are derived from taking risks – and it is preferable to be 'approximately correct, rather than precisely wrong'. The risk assessment process should also allow for the possibility of unexpected positive outcomes, or what the Standard calls "opportunities". Risks are analysed in terms of their likelihood of occurrence and their impact if they do. The impact can be either positive or negative. Different organisations have different thresholds for what they consider acceptable – what they can live with – regarding likelihood and impact, and this threshold must be defined in terms of risk acceptance criteria.

Risk workshop

One way to perform the risk assessment (having first defined and documented the risk assessment process) is to hold a risk workshop. The starting point for this workshop would be for the lead risk assessor to create a list of relevant risks that would compromise the confidentiality, integrity and availability of information that is within the scope of the management system, and which roles within the organisation might own each of those risks.

The risk workshop would be convened and managed by the lead risk assessor and would involve all the risk owners from across the business. The role of the risk workshop is to ensure that the list of identified risks (and relevant opportunities) is complete, that risk owners have been appropriately assigned, to determine the likelihood and impact of each of the identified risks, and to evaluate those risks against the identified risk acceptance criteria.

Impacts

Identify the possible impacts that the occurrence of a risk event will have on an information asset's availability, confidentiality or integrity (impact analysis). These impacts should all, wherever possible, be assigned an estimated monetary value, using a category system (e.g. less than £1k, between £1k and £10k, etc.) that reflects the size of the organisation and the total cost (direct and indirect) of the incident.

Assess the probability of the event occurring, using a classification system such as once every few years, once per year, once every six months, etc. Virus attacks would fall into the every day category.

This enables you to identify the level of risk (pragmatically, a low-medium-high classification for the impact and likelihood scales is usually adequate for a smaller organisation) and then to conclude, for each risk, and in the light of controls already in place, whether it is acceptable or if some form of additional control is required.

Controls

Your risk assessment drives your selection of controls over and above those that might fall within what I have called the baseline control set. The key thing to bear in mind about the risk assessment is that it is not a once-only exercise. You will need to repeat it on a regular basis, just to check that your baseline assessment is still accurate and that the controls you have deployed are still appropriate. You will need to carry out specific risk assessments on an ongoing basis whenever there is a change in circumstances, in business structure or environment, or in the risk profile. Every decision you make about the controls that you are going to deploy must be driven by your risk assessment.

Your approach to risk assessment will be a cornerstone of your ISMS. That is why many organisations use risk assessment tools as part of their management system.

Risk assessment tools

Most organisations will want to automate their risk assessment process so that this best practice becomes embedded in the organisation. This is most easily done by acquiring and using a standard ISO 27001 risk assessment software tool. The benefits of automation show through early on in terms of simplifying the actual risk assessment; the long term benefits are even greater because of the extent to which automation makes the process of review and maintenance so much more robust.

vsRisk™ is a software tool developed specifically for the automation of ISO 27001 risk assessments. You can read more about vsRisk™ here: *www.vigilantsoftware.co.uk*

Controls

The risk assessment is at the heart of the ISMS, as the controls adopted by the organisation will form a significant part of the completed system. The reality is that a significant part of the project time will be invested in designing, deploying, testing and revising appropriate controls that are intended to meet the identified risks. It is therefore important to have an overview of controls.

The concepts of *risks* and *controls* are linked and are fundamental to information security management systems. Risk might be defined as 'the combination of the probability of an event and its consequences'. Control is defined in ISO/IEC 27000 as a "means of managing risk"; a control includes policies, procedures, guidelines, practices or organisational structures – these can be of an administrative, technical, management or legal nature. Please note that information security controls are not simply technical in nature. If they were simply technical, they would fail – if only because no control can implement and maintain itself autonomously.

Nature of controls

All information security controls are made up of a mix of process/procedure, technology and human activity. Looking, for example, at the virus and cyber threats that are widely recognised even by boards of directors, ISO 27001 Control A.12.2.1 – and common sense - require the implementation of controls against malicious software and, when you think about this issue, it is immediately clear that technological controls must be blended with procedural ones – neither on its own is adequate. It is also clear that malware that corrupts a system is not only a business continuity and reputational issue – it may also corrupt records that need to be retained or make it impossible for an organisation to complete or submit required reports on time:

At the same time, ISO 27001 Control A.13.2.3 requires that information "involved in electronic messaging shall be appropriately protected". Anti-malware software, on its own, just doesn't meet a requirement that clearly covers both email and instant messaging. What you need, according to both common sense and ISO 27001, is a mix of technology, process and correct behaviour.

Yes, you need an appropriate software package, one that will ensure that incoming viruses, worms and Trojans are stopped at the perimeter – and that spam is filtered out – but it's no good if documents that users have specifically requested from external sources and that are coming by email are corrupted by the anti-malware software 'just in case' – we know, for instance, that pdfs sent via an automatic response e-marketer are often nuked by the recipient organisation's anti-malware software and that the same document, when sent individually to the recipient, will pass through with little problem – this sort of software set-up promotes disrespect among its users and a tendency to try and bypass it, potentially with attachments that are really dangerous. Instant messaging has become one of the simplest ways for individuals to circumvent email restrictions and ISO 27001 now expects those risks to be identified and controlled.

End-point security is now also a huge issue – traditionally, the organisational information security perimeter was easy to define and defend, but with the proliferation of hand held devices, wireless networks and mobile working, the perimeter has become very hard to defend and very porous. Depending on the risk assessment, organisations need to be looking at software that will tackle the risks in handhelds rather than making them difficult to deploy. Wireless networks need to be properly set up – and mobile access should be by means of an appropriately secure connection, probably a VPN. This control area will be found to interact with Control A.6.2, which requires the organisation to have a formal policy and appropriate controls in place to protect against the risks of working with mobile computing facilities.

Of course, anti-malware software needs to work with the firewall seamlessly, and it goes out of date – fast – so you need to have procedures in place that ensure it is properly updated. Most organisations don't have a lot of time for testing anti-malware or other updates and fixes. Nevertheless, exploits and attacks have revealed vulnerabilities are now happening faster and faster – rapid deployment of fixes is usually critical, and this can only be achieved if you've got the right structures and processes in place.

In addition, your staff need to be trained on what to do when there is an incident – whether that is an email virus, a hoax or someone uploading something from a USB stick. And when it all goes wrong (as, sooner or later, it inevitably will), you need to have put in place ways of keeping the ship afloat while you plug the holes.

Control selection criteria

You should only deploy controls that relate to, and are appropriate and in proportion to, the actual risks you face. While you can choose controls from any source you consider appropriate, ISO 27001:2013 requires that you compare any controls that you do select against its own list of the key best-practice controls relating to the whole range of potential risks (many of which your organisation may not face). The Standard also requires inclusions and exclusions to be justified.

Controls can be described as 'countermeasures for risks'. Apart from knowingly accepting risks that fall within the (board-determined) criteria of acceptability, or transferring those risks (through insurance) to others, there are three types of control:

1. Preventative controls protect vulnerabilities and make an attack unsuccessful or reduce its impact.

2. Corrective controls reduce the effect of an attack.
3. Detective controls discover attacks and trigger preventative or corrective controls.

Controls are not implemented irrespective of the cost. No board should sign off on any ISMS proposal that seeks to remove all risk from the business – the business does, after all, exist within a risk framework and, as the only form of existence that is completely risk-free involves already being dead, there is little point in proposing to control every risk.

It is essential that any controls that are implemented are cost-effective. The principle is that the cost of implementing and maintaining a control should be no greater than the identified and quantified cost of the impact of the identified threat (or threats). It is not possible to provide total security against every single risk; the trade-off involves providing effective security against most risks.

No organisation should invest in information security technology (hardware or software), or implement information security management processes and procedures, without having carried out an appropriate risk assessment that assures them that:

• The proposed investment (the total cost of the control) is the same as, or less than, the cost of the identified threat's impact;

• The risk classification, which takes into account its probability, is appropriate for the proposed investment; and

• The priority of the risk has been considered – i.e. all the risks with higher prioritisations have already been adequately controlled and, therefore, it is now appropriate to invest in controlling this one.

If the organisation cannot satisfy itself that the proposed investment meets these criteria, it will be wasting both the money and the time required to implement the control, while leaving itself open to more likely risks and, conceivably, with inadequate resources to respond to the more likely risk when it occurs. There is, in other words, a risk associated with not carrying out – and maintaining – an adequate risk assessment.

Statement of applicability

The second most important document in your ISMS – after the information security policy statement itself – is your Statement of Applicability, or SoA. The SoA is, in essence, a list of all the controls identified in Annex A of ISO/IEC 27001:2013, together with your statement as to whether or not that control is applied in your organisation, the justification for its inclusion or exclusion, a statement as to whether or not the control is required and whether it has actually been implemented or not. The SoA also includes controls selected from other sources, if you have any.

Risk treatment decisions – accept the risk, reject it, transfer it through insurance or control it, also described as 'Retain, Avoid, Share and Modify' – have to be made for each risk on the basis of the organisation's pre-determined risk appetite and within the context of the risk assessment framework. Risk treatment decisions must be justified by the risk assessment (recognise the baseline controls required to meet legal, regulatory and contractual objectives) and each control should be proportionate to the identified risk.

ISO/IEC 27002 has the status of a code of practice and it provides detailed guidance on how to implement each of the 114 controls listed in Annex A of ISO/IEC 27001.

The best detailed guidance that exists on the market today, and which tackles the SoA on a control by control basis, is *IT Governance – An International Guide to Data Security and ISO27001/ISO27002, Sixth Edition*, which was chosen as The Open University's post graduate text book precisely because of the quality of its coverage of this core component of the ISMS. Whether you're using consultants for your project or not, you will find this book indispensable[1] to your ISMS project.

Risk treatment plan

The next most important document, after the SoA, is the Risk Treatment Plan (RTP). This sets out the steps to be taken to deal with each of the risks you identified in your risk assessment. Those risks that you are accepting or rejecting need no further action other than possibly finding a workaround for those you reject. Those that are being transferred need to be the subject of negotiations with insurers and/or suppliers. Those that are to be controlled need action, and your RTP describes those actions: what has to be done, by whom and by when.

---

[1] While I am one of the co-authors of this book, the fact is that there is nothing like it on the market.

CHAPTER 7: IMPLEMENTATION

The seventh of the nine steps deals primarily with the implementation of the Risk Treatment Plan – putting in place the selected information security controls. The technical aspects of control implementation – re-configuring firewalls, implementing boot-level encryption on laptops, segregating networks, meeting DPA or PCI compliance requirements, and so on – all depend in the first instance on the competence of those charged with the implementation.

The focal points of this step, therefore, are the competence of those in the information security team, as well as of others across the organisation who will be responsible for documenting processes, for communication about changed processes and controls across the organisation, and for staff awareness, training and education. At this point, you will also deal with outsourced processes.

Competencies

You will need a process to determine, review, and maintain the competencies necessary to achieve your ISMS objectives. Competence is defined in ISO 27000:2014 as the "ability to apply knowledge and skills to achieve the intended results". But what competencies do you need?

To answer this question, you should conduct a needs analysis, assessing the competencies required for the effective management of the ISMS. The organisation has to define competence, either in terms of experience or in terms of qualifications. The current reality is that there are relatively small numbers of people who have meaningful

ISO 27001 experience and, therefore, organisations tend to default to formal qualifications as a way of determining and assessing competence. We have looked at this previously: information security lead implementer, lead ISMS auditor and internal ISMS auditor are typical competencies required, and IBITGQ qualifications in these subjects are typical ways that organisations demonstrate they have acquired what they need.

Information security requires more than just implementation and audit competencies, though. It also requires competence in areas like risk assessment, business continuity and incident management, as well as in more technical areas such as security testing, network security architectures, and so on. Qualifications like CISMP, CISSP, CEH and CISM are becoming more common among information security professionals, but you also need to consider specific qualifications, such as those for managing Microsoft or Cisco security, or PKI infrastructure, for instance.

Once you've determined the competencies required for your ISMS, you need to acquire them – either through recruitment, sub-contracting or, more practically, by getting your existing staff trained and qualified. Public training organisations (such as the training arm of IT Governance Ltd) offer these sorts of training courses and access to the associated exams.

Evidence of competence needs to be retained. The most appropriate place in which to do this is individual HR files.

The 'all persons' requirement

It is a requirement of the Standard that all "persons under the organisation's control" are appropriately aware of the information security policy, the ISMS – and their contribution to it – as well as the implications of not conforming with ISMS requirements. The group of persons to whom this applies would logically include, as well as employees, all associates and contractors doing work either on behalf of the organisation or within its security perimeter, ranging from cleaners through to network support engineers.

While it is relatively straightforward to make this work in respect of staff and direct contractors, it is somewhat harder when dealing with those indirectly contracted to do work under the organisation's control; cleaners and network engineers, employed by a third party that has a specific service contract with your organisation, could be under your control when on your premises; you need to build into supplier contracts an obligation to ensure that their staff comply with this requirement – and then make it possible for them to do so.

Staff awareness

It is also a requirement of the Standard that all staff should receive training in relation to the ISMS and that their awareness of the ISMS and information security issues should be maintained over time. This is perfectly sensible; staff can be most organisations' weakest link and, in an era where 'hacking the human' is just one of the standard skill sets of most cyber attackers, the humans on your staff need to be on their guard at all times. Of course, there is also the possibility that staff can make errors – inputting data, for instance – that could have outcomes as catastrophic as a major cyber attack.

Practically speaking, this means that staff need basic training – when they join the organisation – on how the IT systems operate and what their obligations are regarding information security. Most staff should also sign an acceptable use agreement when they join the organisation, and this document should set out in detail all aspects of the expected behaviours, from password strength through to clean desk and clear screen policies and protection of PII. Initial staff training should, at the very least, cover all the acceptable use requirements, as well as the policies and procedures the user is expected to comply with.

Refresher training should be provided on a regular basis; this refresher training can cover the same area as the original training, or it can be varied and updated to reflect a changing risk environment. As you're looking for continued compliance with your acceptable use agreement, there is some sense in re-delivering the same core training.

There are three challenges with the traditional way of delivering such training, which is some form of group session. The first is that it is expensive in terms of trainer and staff time. The second is that, invariably, not everyone manages to attend the training – and it's the person who doesn't attend who's likely to cause the problem. The third is that you usually can't extract evidence from this kind of training that everyone paid attention and learnt what they were intended to learn; for a successful court case, you might need to be able to demonstrate that a transgressor was actually aware that their actions were wrong.

Increasingly, organisations address these challenges through e-learning – staff awareness training delivered online. Typically, a 40-minute staff awareness training course can be delivered cost-effectively and consistently to everyone within an organisation within a specific time frame. As everyone does the training at a time to suit them, you can ensure that everyone does get trained. Everyone gets the same message. And you can attach tests to the training, so you have evidence that people learnt what they were meant to learn. The most important aspect of online compliance staff awareness training is the extent of the administrative reporting; the interactivity of the course itself is far less important, and this has the benefit that you can usually keep down the cost of delivering this sort of training – either from a cloud provider or through your own in-house learning management system.

IT Governance is one of a number of organisations that can provide online ISO 27001 staff awareness training to help address this need.

Of course, staff awareness training often dovetails with the organisation's communication strategy; keeping staff up-to-date with information security awareness is, in practical terms, simply building on the initial and repeat core training, and should be fundamental to how you keep staff aware of the dangers of a wide variety of social engineering-type attacks.

Outsourced processes

ISO 27001 specifies that outsourced processes must fall within the scope of the ISMS, even though the organisation delivering that process is by definition outside the scope. An outsourced process is one where the organisation has contracted with a third party to manage or operate a service on its behalf, such as desktop support. An outsourced service is not necessarily the same thing as a bought-in service; while you are able to determine how an outsourced service is operated, you have little discretion about bought-in ones.

Processes that fall within the scope of the ISMS must be controlled. Typically, outsourced processes are controlled through some mix of:

- terms and conditions of contract;
- supplier information security questionnaires;
- mandating and monitoring recognised assurance badges; and/or
- supplier audits.

CHAPTER 8: MEASURE, MONITOR AND REVIEW

A useful ISMS is one that helps an organisation achieve its information security objectives – those objectives should be linked to its business, regulatory and contractual objectives and should be delegated to appropriate levels within the organisation.

ISO 27001 requires the organisation "to continually improve the suitability, adequacy and effectiveness of the ISMS". The corrective action requirements of the Standard are met by an effective ISMS audit plan, competent review of non-conformities (part of the responsibility of the information security manager), the incident response procedures and the related documentation.

The combination of effective monitoring, measuring, and corrective action processes – together with a formal review process and strong internal audit structure – within the context of an ISMS will enable an organisation to start driving continual improvement through the organisation. (Of course, if the original approach to the ISMS implementation was to structure it as a continual security improvement project, then this concept will already be built into the underlying logic of the ISMS.)

A long-term approach to continual improvement should include measuring the effectiveness of the ISMS and of the processes and controls that have been adopted. ISO 27001 requires effectiveness measurements, and for the results from these to be included in the input to the management review meeting. Clearly, information security as an organisational function needs to be measured against performance targets in just the same way as other parts of the organisation. The organisation also needs to be able to measure progress toward its corporate security objectives, and this is also a requirement of ISO 27001.

In order to develop a useful set of metrics, an organisation will have to identify what to measure, how to measure it and when to measure it.

Key areas that should be considered for their contribution to the organisation's ISMS goals and key objectives should include:

- Effectiveness of identified controls and groups of controls that relate to the most significant risks identified in the risk assessment.
- Effectiveness and cost-effectiveness of the organisation's information security awareness, education and training.
- Extent and effectiveness of vulnerability patching and management.
- Improvement in efficiency generated by access controls and external contracts.
- Effectiveness of the incident handling process.
- Effectiveness of perimeter security and speed of remediation through penetration testing.

Internal audit, and testing

ISO 27001 requires that internal audits of the ISMS are conducted at planned intervals.

Your ISMS has to work in the real world. You've identified risks, you've deployed what appear to be appropriate controls, and you want to be sure of two things: first, that the controls work as intended and, second, that when they are overwhelmed (as, sooner or later, they will be) your emergency counter-measures also work. Your management system, including each and every control, is planned and deployed, the management system and every control are then tested to see if they work according to plan, and the management system and every control are improved in light of that testing.

There are four types of testing that should be considered. The first is internal audit, which involves a trained ISMS auditor taking a documented procedure and asking for evidence that what is described in the procedure is what actually happens. As part of your ISMS project, you will need to put a team of trained ISMS internal auditors in place. These people can be drawn from around the business, appropriately trained and, provided you ensure that they never audit any part of the business for which they – or their managers – are responsible, they will meet your long term audit team requirements.

The second is a limited 'paper test'. This is an intellectual exercise; it requires more than one person, and also requires familiarity with the vulnerabilities in the asset, the mechanisms of the control and the mechanisms and makeup of the likely threats. Given this knowledge – which should be both current and experientially and technically based – the effectiveness of controls (such as incident management or business continuity controls) can be logically tested.

The third is a limited, real-life test. This could, for instance, involve powering down the server room during normal operations to find out whether the APS systems and server shut-down procedures all worked as specified. Real-life tests should not be carried out without first having taken extensive steps to ensure that, if something doesn't work as planned, the system can be restored to the point it was at when the test was executed. This type of testing includes penetration testing, which should be carried out by a specialist penetration testing firm, and should test both your selected controls and your risk assessment: in other words, you should instruct your penetration tester to try and penetrate your system by methods that you haven't identified. You can later assess whether these are threats against which you need to control.

The fourth and final type of test is a large scale scenario test, most usually used to test major cyber incident and business continuity plans. These tests usually try and telescope the events of several days into a much shorter space of time and require all those who would have roles in the real-life disaster to attempt to perform the required tasks in the role play. These tests require considerable planning and, again, it is a sensible area in which to deploy external, specialist expertise.

You will need to schedule audits and tests so that all aspects of your ISMS are covered in the course of a year. You will need to do this on the basis that some controls will need to be tested more regularly than others; you should carry out a risk assessment to determine the frequency of testing that you will require. Your external certification auditors will want to see evidence of your internal audit and testing, the results of this activity, and details of how you have used the findings of this activity to improve and tighten your ISMS. You should assume that your external certification auditor will want to see evidence of at least one cycle of audits and tests. If you want to achieve certification after less than one year's worth of testing, you will need to design a test and audit cycle that covers all the mission critical aspects of your ISMS within a much shorter time frame. This is not an unusual approach and most certification bodies should accept that there are a number of items that do not need to be tested that regularly.

Management review

Top management should review the performance of the ISMS on at least an annual basis. Inputs to the management review process will include all the results from internal audits and testing, as well as continual improvement activity and analysis of non-conformances and incidents that have occurred during the preceding period. As I have said elsewhere, root cause analysis is the preferred approach.

The management review should look inwards at the performance of the management system, and at the metrics that describe how the ISMS is performing in relation to its objectives; it should also look outwards at the world in which the organisation operates, to ensure that it is taking appropriate steps in the context of changes to its operating and risk environment.

CHAPTER 9: CERTIFICATION

While your selection of certification body should have no impact on your success in achieving certification, there are a couple of issues you should consider in making your selection – which isn't necessary until you have already made considerable progress toward readiness for certification. You will, of course, want to ensure that there is a cultural fit between yourself and your supplier of certification services, and that pricing and so on is acceptable.

There are two other key issues that do need to be taken into account when making this selection: the first is relevant to organisations that already have one or more externally certified management systems in place, the second applies specifically to organisations tackling ISO 27001.

It is essential that your ISMS is fully integrated into your organisation; it will not work effectively if it is a separate management system and exists outside of, and parallel, to any other management systems. Logically, this means that the framework, processes and controls of the ISMS must be integrated with, for instance, your ISO 9001 quality system to the greatest extent possible. Clearly, therefore, assessment of your management systems must also be integrated: you want one audit that deals with all the aspects of your management system. Doing anything else is simply too disruptive to the organisation, too costly and too destructive to good business practice. You should ensure that whoever you choose for your ISMS audit can, and does, offer an integrated assessment service.

The second issue that you should take into account when selecting your supplier of certification services is their approach to certification itself. An ISMS is fundamentally designed to reflect the organisation's assessment of risks in and around information security. In other words, each ISMS will be different. It is important, therefore, that each external assessment of an ISMS takes that difference into account so that the client gets an assessment that *adds value* to its business, rather than one that is merely a mechanical comparison of the ISMS against the requirements of ISO 27001.

Once you have chosen your certification body and you are ready for a certification audit, there are six secrets to certification success. None of these secrets will get you through an audit that you are fundamentally not ready for, nor will they enable an inadequate ISMS to achieve certification. However, they do ensure that all the good aspects of your ISMS are noted and that the auditors are left with a favourable overall impression.

1. Impress the auditors as early as possible by ensuring that your documentation is complete, comprehensive and all available for inspection at the initial visit – the one that comes before the actual certification audit. This first visit is expressly to determine if your ISMS is ready for external audit.

2. Ensure that all your internal audit and testing records are immediately available for the certification auditors when they plan and commence their work; they should use these records to focus their attention on key areas of the ISMS, so ensure that you have adequately tested them. No external auditor wants to sign off on a system that is breached a week later, and the thoroughness of your own work will give the auditor confidence.

3. Teach staff throughout the organisation to be completely open and honest with the auditors, especially about things they feel may not be up to standard. This serves two

purposes: it flushes out weaknesses that you can tighten up on, and it demonstrates to the auditors that you have an open organisation that identifies and deals with information security issues. By contrast, an attempt to suggest that everything is perfect throughout the organisation will provoke incredulity amongst the auditors; they have learned, through long experience, that no system is without flaws and that every attempt to pretend to perfection hides a myriad of previously undetected imperfections. Do not encourage them to start hunting these imperfections down.

4. Teach staff who are likely to be interviewed by auditors to show how the system that is being examined actually works, and to restrict what they say to answering the specific questions asked without explaining anything off-topic. This will demonstrate to the auditor that your people are tightly focused, and will also avoid the danger of someone talking so much that they lead the auditor to examine an aspect of your ISMS that doesn't need external examination.

5. Critically, ensure that management are fully involved in the certification audit. If necessary, rehearse with senior management the type of questions that they will be asked and the types of answers that they will be expected to give. While senior management should be perfectly capable of handling the audit (as they will have been involved in and fully committed to the ISMS project from the outset) they may not be fully aware of how best to demonstrate this commitment to an external auditor. Done well, senior management's performance on the day can make a substantial contribution to certification success.

6. Be prepared to argue. You should do this only in a constructive and calm fashion, but if there are issues on

which you feel that an auditor has misunderstood your ISMS or some aspect of it, or has misinterpreted the Standard, and is, as a result, thinking about recording a non-conformity (either major or minor), you should set out, calmly and firmly, why you believe that you are in the right. Auditors will respond negatively to any attempt to browbeat or belittle them; they will (usually) respond positively to any constructive attempt to help them achieve a better outcome. And the greater their conviction that you're committed to the long-term effectiveness of your ISMS, the more prepared they will be to give you the benefit of the doubt on any marginal decisions.

The outcome of the initial audit should, if the organisation has diligently followed all the recommendations contained in this book, be certification of the ISMS to ISO 27001 and the issuing of a certificate setting this out. The certificate should be appropriately displayed and the organisation should start preparing for its first surveillance visit, which will take place about six to nine months later. Any minor non-conformances should be capable of being closed out by email, and any recommendation for certification will be dependent on this happening within an agreed timescale.

The certificate will refer to the latest version of the SoA and the auditors will check for updates on their subsequent visits. Therefore, when supplying a copy of the certificate to clients, stakeholders or other parties, the organisation should be prepared to provide a copy of the most recent SoA. While the SoA is a living document, updated as and when necessary, the organisation should endeavour to keep such updates and alterations to a minimum.

ISO 27001 RESOURCES

ISO 27001:2013 ISMS Documentation Toolkit

Overview

The ISO 27001:2013 ISMS Documentation Toolkit has been developed by our leading ISO 27001 experts, compiling real-world practice and experience into easy-to-use document templates.

This documentation toolkit will accelerate any ISMS project, reducing costs and stress, while still reflecting any corporate style and branding.

Benefits

- Accelerate your management system implementation, saving you time and money.

- Provide your interested parties with evidence that risks have been adequately addressed.

- Ensure nothing is left out of your ISMS documentation.

- Streamline compliance with ISO 27001:2013, making it easier and simpler for you and your team.

- Reduce the room for error and time-wasting when developing your own templates.

- Block off potential project dead ends.

- Easily integrate your ISMS documentation with your business processes.

Features

- Fully customisable;
- Integrates with risk assessment tool vsRisk™;
- Provides complete coverage of ISO 27001:2013;
- One-time automation input to handle repeated information.

Download a free toolkit trial here:

www.itgovernance.co.uk/integrated-management-systems/iso27001-toolkit.aspx

vsRisk™

Overview

vsRisk™ enables organisations to conduct hassle-free information security risk assessments according to the requirements of ISO 27001 by providing the framework, database and resources needed for the job. vsRisk™ simplifies and speeds up the risk assessment process, cuts costs and ensures accurate, repeatable risk assessments, year after year.

Benefits

- Minimises the hassle and complexity of carrying out an information security risk assessment, saving time and resources.
- Ensures accurate results and enables risk assessments to be repeated year after year.
- Meets ISO 27001 requirements for consistent risk assessments.

- Accelerates control implementation with the integrated ISMS Documentation Toolkit.
- Contains cross-maps to all leading control frameworks.
- Generates reports for exporting, editing and sharing across the business and with auditors – including the SoA and RTP.

Features

- Track risks, actions and priorities from dashboard views.
- Apply data from two built-in databases:
  o Threats and vulnerabilities
  o Seven different control sets (ISO 27001 (2005 and 2013), NIST SP 800-53, Cloud Controls Matrix, PCI DSS, Cyber Essentials, ISO 27032).
- Copy, edit and replicate a built-in sample risk assessment.
- Upload policies or procedures for controls straight from an ISO 27001 documentation toolkit.
- Apply implementation details.
- Collaborate with multiple users or assessors.
- Add comments and deadlines.
- Add or clone additional ISMSs.
- Draw, edit and print instant, audit-ready reports.

View the product details here:

vsRisk Standalone:
www.itgovernance.co.uk/shop/p-1228-vsrisk-standalone-basic.aspx

vsRisk Multi-user:
www.itgovernance.co.uk/shop/p-1534-vsrisk-multi-user-
full.aspx

Free demo

A free personal demonstration of the software can be arranged.

(UK) IT Legal Compliance Database

Overview

The IT Legal Compliance Database is a comprehensive, simple and user-friendly legal compliance service to help you implement and comply with ISO 27001. ISO 27001 requires you to develop an ISMS taking into account "the requirements of […] interested parties [including] legal and regulatory requirements and contractual obligations" (Clause 4.2). The only cost-effective and straightforward way to ensure you meet these legal and regulatory requirements is with the (UK) IT Legal Compliance Database.

Benefits

- A user-friendly, cost-effective and comprehensive tool to ensure compliance with key laws and their associated information security clauses.

- Saves time, hassle and the expense of trying to find, review and interpret the legal requirements as they will apply to your ISMS.

- Provides auditors with a concise overview of an organisation's compliance status against each piece of relevant legislation.

- Enables organisations to remain abreast of legislative changes by receiving regular updates on an annual subscription contract, ensuring the organisation is always compliant.

Features

- Access an updated list of over 90 statutes and regulations for England and Wales.

- Select the applicable laws and regulations as they relate to information security and to your own business environment.

- Review full-text versions of relevant clauses for the listed laws and regulations.

- View recommended controls from ISO 27001:2013 and ISO 27001:2005 for each clause.

- Simply drag and drop to select or remove controls.

- Record and update your compliance status against each clause.

- View specific implementation requirements as they relate to each clause.

- Apply filters to view a specific set of clauses or compliance requirements.

- View the enforcement bodies for each piece of legislation.

View the product details here:

www.itgovernance.co.uk/shop/p-715-uk-it-legal-compliance-database.aspx

ISO 27001 staff awareness e-learning

Overview

This e-learning course enables employees to gain a better understanding of information security risks and compliance 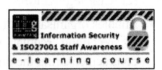 requirements in line with ISO 27001:2013, thereby reducing the organisation's exposure to security threats. Using IT Governance's substantial experience in consulting and training, this course is set out to meet the requirements of ISO 27001:2013, which specifies that it is imperative to address security issues at the employee level.

Benefits

- The use of non-technical language ensures the contents are understood by all staff.

- The course provides systematic, consistent and repeatable training across multiple learners.

- Simple to use with relevant and informative content.

- Enables basic yet fundamental training on information security and ISO 27001:2013, reducing the organisation's liability due to security failures.

- Provides comprehensive reports as evidence that training has actually been provided.

- Can be deployed for existing employees and as part of an induction process for new hires.

Course overview

- What is information security and what does it have to do with you?
- Where does your organisation fit in?
- Could this happen to you? (Scenarios and follow up questions);
- An overview of the concept of an information security management system;
- Information security at home;
- Information security at work;
- Potential weaknesses: passwords, phishing, social media, USB sticks, sat nav, secure perimeters, tailgating, clear desk and screen;
- Information classification;
- Intellectual property;
- Security incidents;
- Business continuity;
- Key policies and procedures.

Other Information

The course includes an online test and certificate. The course can be customised upon request, and can be hosted externally (from our online e-hosting learning environment) or internally (from your own network environment).

View the course details here:

www.itgovernance.co.uk/shop/p-792-information-security-iso27001-staff-awareness-e-learning-course.aspx

ISO27001 Do It Yourself packaged consultancy

Overview

A complete set of resources designed to help organisations implement an information security management system aligned with ISO 27001.

Benefits

- Get comprehensive tools and guidance from the experts in ISO 27001.
- Take control of your own project by implementing an ISO 27001-compliant ISMS.
- Avoid costly consultancy fees and implement the Standard at a budget.
- Empower yourself and your team to retain the needed skills for implementing ISO 27001.
- Get detailed implementation advice based on practical experience.
- Access all the resources in your own time and at your own pace.
- Use the tools to reduce the time and effort required to implement a management system.

Features

Three international standards, essential as a reference for implementing the Standard:

- The ISO 27001:2013 standard
- The ISO 27002:2013 standard

- The ISO 27000:2014 standard

Two bestselling implementation guides, delivering practical implementation guidance:

- *IT Governance – An International Guide to Data Security and ISO27001/ISO27002*
- *Nine Steps to Success – An ISO 27001 Implementation Overview*

Proven tools to save time and money:

- vsRisk™ – the definitive cyber security risk assessment tool
- The ISO 27001 Documentation Toolkit

View the package details here:

www.itgovernance.co.uk/shop/p-1684-iso27001-do-it-yourself-package.aspx

ISO 27001 Get A Little Help packaged consultancy

Overview

This package contains the core ISO 27001 standards, two bestselling ISO 27001 implementation guidance manuals, implementation tools, and places on our Live Online Lead Implementer and Lead Auditor training courses.

Get A Little Help
ISO 27001

Benefits

- Take advantage of a comprehensive blend of training, tools, online consultancy and software.

- Save money by implementing ISO 27001 without the added expense of consultancy.
- Tackle each step of your ISO 27001 implementation project with expert guidance, training and best-in-class tools.
- Enables companies with little or no experience of management systems to get started with implementing ISO 27001.
- Avoid costly consultancy fees and implement the Standard on a budget.
- Empower yourself and your team to retain the needed skills for implementing ISO 27001.
- Get detailed implementation advice based on practical experience.
- Access all the resources in your own time and at your own pace.

Features

The package includes the following:

Live Online consultancy support:

- Two hours of Live Online expert consultancy support on specific issues.

Three international standards, essential as a reference for implementing the Standard:

- The ISO 27001:2013 standard
- The ISO 27002:2013 standard
- The ISO 27000:2014 standard

Two bestselling implementation guides, delivering practical implementation guidance:

- *IT Governance – An International Guide to Data Security and ISO27001/ISO27002*
- *Nine Steps to Success – An ISO 27001 Implementation Overview*

Critical skills training, delivered conveniently online:

- ISO 27001 Certified ISMS Lead Implementer Online Masterclass
- ISO 27001 Certified ISMS Lead Auditor Online Masterclass

Proven tools to save time and money:

- vsRisk™ – the definitive cyber security risk assessment tool
- The ISO 27001 Documentation Toolkit

View the package details here:

www.itgovernance.co.uk/shop/p-1651-iso27001-get-a-little-help-package.aspx

ISO 27001 Get A Lot Of Help packaged consultancy

Overview

This package contains five days of structured, expert online consultancy, including the core ISO 27001 standards, two bestselling ISO 27001 implementation guidance manuals, implementation tools, and places on our Live Online lead implementer and lead auditor training courses.

Benefits

- You get a range of expertly developed tools and resources to help you fulfil your ISO 27001 implementation requirements.

- We help you set the project framework and timelines so that you can manage the execution of the deliverables according to your own needs.

- You benefit from the personal leadership of, and knowledge transfer from, your implementation coach.

- The costs of extensive consultancy work, travelling and other expenses are totally eliminated.

- Appointments take place at flexible times and at a location convenient to you and your team.

- Where needed, our consultants can arrange for additional support for your project, which will be billed separately and agreed up front.

Features

The package includes the following:

- Mentor and coach consultancy
  Five days of structured consultancy to ensure that the planning and implementation of the project stays on track and achieves its implementation goals. It is delivered online by expert practitioners.

Plus the following critical tools, training courses and guides:

- Three international standards, essential as a reference for implementing the standard

- *IT Governance – An International Guide to Data Security and ISO27001/ISO27002* Book
- *Nine Steps to Success – An ISO 27001 Implementation Overview* Guide
- Three-day ISO 27001 Certified ISMS Lead Implementer Online Masterclass
- Five-day ISO 27001 Certified ISMS Lead Auditor Online Masterclass
- vsRisk™ – the definitive cyber security risk assessment tool
- The ISO 27001 Documentation Toolkit

View the package details here:

www.itgovernance.co.uk/shop/p-1650-iso27001-get-a-lot-of-help-package.aspx

ISO 27001 bespoke consultancy

Overview

Whatever an organisation's ISO/IEC 27001 consultancy needs, IT Governance has the right level of service – from fixed-price packages to a comprehensive range of bespoke services that will help you successfully implement an ISO 27001-compliant information security management system (ISMS) – 100% certification guaranteed.

All of our ISO 27001 consultancy services can be delivered online to reduce consultancy fees and ensure optimal return on investment.

Why thousands of companies trust us for ISO 27001 advice:

- Enjoy the peace of mind that your project is in the hands of the world's ISO 27001 experts.
- Receive a 100% guarantee of successful certification.
- Benefit from pragmatic, proven and straightforward implementation approach.
- Receive support developing a business case to secure the necessary information security investment.
- Maintain control over your ISMS – you receive the knowledge to maintain the ISMS following certification.
- Choose from the most exhaustive range of ISO 27001 tools, books and training courses in the world.
- Use the certification body of your choice – we support independent accredited certification.
- Select the best fit for your needs and objectives – we're independent of vendors and certification bodies.
- Our management standards expertise means we can help with much more than a single project.

Consultancy services

IT Governance delivers the full range of support required to achieve ISO 27001 certification, including the following popular services:

- **ISO 27001 Gap Analysis**
  This expert, in-person review of your information security arrangements against the requirements of ISO/IEC 27001:2013 is ideal for organisations seeking

to develop a business case and secure budget approval for implementing an ISO 27001-aligned ISMS.

- **ISO 27001 FastTrack™**
  A fixed-price online consultancy package designed to help small organisations reach ISO 27001 certification readiness in just three months. Available either as an in-person consultancy or online service.

View further details of our ISO 27001 consultancy services here:

www.itgovernance.co.uk/iso27001_consultancy.aspx

ISO 27001 Certified ISMS Lead Implementer Training Course

Overview

This three-day course covers all of the key steps involved in planning, implementing and maintaining an ISO 27001-compliant information security management system (ISMS). Delegates who pass the included exam are awarded the ISO 27001 Certified ISMS Lead Implementer (CIS LI) qualification issued by the International Board for IT Governance Qualifications (IBITGQ).

This course is also delivered in-house or Live Online

Save time and travel costs with training delivered to any location with Internet access.

What will delegates learn?

- Securing senior management commitment and building the business case;

- The role and structure of an information security policy;
- How to determine the scope of your ISMS based on the requirements of ISO 27001;
- Developing a management framework.
- How to structure and manage your ISO 27001 project;
- How to allocate roles and responsibilities for your ISO 27001 implementation;
- The definition of risk in ISO 27001 and options for risk assessments under the Standard;
- The benefits of, and key issues when selecting, a risk assessment tool;
- How to carry out an information security risk assessment – the core competence of information security management;
- The Statement of Applicability (SoA), and justifications for inclusions and exclusions;
- Reviewing your existing controls and mapping controls to Annex A of ISO 27001;
- How to manage and drive continual improvement under ISO 27001;
- How to prepare for your ISO 27001 certification audit.

View further details here:

www.itgovernance.co.uk/shop/p-713-iso27001-certified-isms-lead-implementer.aspx

The online version is available here:

www.itgovernance.co.uk/shop/p-714-iso27001-certified-isms-lead-implementer-online.aspx

ISO 27001 Certified ISMS Lead Auditor Training Course

Overview

This course will teach attendees how to plan and execute an ISO 27001 information security management system (ISMS) audit. Delegates who pass the included exam are awarded the ISO 27001 Certified ISMS Lead Auditor (CIS LA) qualification issued by the International Board for IT Governance Qualifications (IBITGQ).

This course is also delivered in-house or Live Online

ISO27001 Lead
Auditor Certificate

Save time and travel costs with training delivered to any location with Internet access

What will delegates learn?

- Best-practice audit methodology based on ISO 19011;
- Preparing, leading and reporting on the findings of an information security audit;
- How to audit an ISMS against ISO 27001;
- Interview techniques, following audit trails, and reviewing and documenting evidence;
- Audit risk assessments, business continuity and continual improvement;
- Identifying nonconformities and ensuring appropriate corrective action is undertaken;
- New audit skills and knowledge, enhanced through role-play exercises, workshops and case study reviews.

View further details here:

www.itgovernance.co.uk/shop/p-712-iso27001-certified-isms-lead-auditor-training-course.aspx

The online version is available here:

www.itgovernance.co.uk/shop/p-1643-iso27001-certified-isms-lead-auditor-online-masterclass.aspx

ISO 27005 Certified Risk Management Training Course

Overview

This course is designed to provide delegates with the knowledge and skills required to undertake an information security risk assessment based on the best-practice guidance outlined in ISO 27005 and fully meeting the requirements of the ISO 27001 standard. Delegates who successfully complete this course will be awarded the ISO 27005 Certified ISMS Risk Management (CIS RM) qualification issued by the International Board for IT Governance Qualifications (IBITGQ).

ISO27005
Risk Management

This course is also delivered in-house

What will delegates learn?

- The role and importance of the risk assessment;
- Why the risk assessment is the core competence of information security management;
- How to use the risk assessment to achieve certification and maintain compliance with the ISO 27001 information security management standard;

- Full details of the ISO/IEC 27005:2011 information risk management standard and an understanding of key risk management terminology;

- How to carry out an effective risk assessment as defined by ISO/IEC 27005:2011, supported by hands-on experience;

- The key information security risk assessment processes, including context establishment, risk assessment, risk treatment and monitoring/review;

- The competence to advise third-party organisations on information security risk assessments.

View further details here:

www.itgovernance.co.uk/shop/p-1309-iso-27005-certified-isms-risk-management.aspx

ITG RESOURCES

IT Governance is a specialist in the field of information security and ISO 27001. We have been involved in designing and successfully implementing cost-effective ISO 27001–compliant information security management systems (ISMSs) since the Standard was first introduced.

We are unique in our ability to provide everything you need in order to implement a best-practice ISMS with the minimum of disruption and difficulty, including standards, tools, books, training, and consultancy and support as detailed in the *ISO 27001 Resources* section.

Publishing Services

IT Governance Publishing (ITGP) is the world's leading IT-GRC publishing imprint that is wholly owned by IT Governance Ltd.

With books and tools covering all IT governance, risk and compliance frameworks, we are the publisher of choice for authors and distributors alike, producing unique and practical publications of the highest quality, in the latest formats available, which readers will find invaluable.

www.itgovernancepublishing.co.uk is the website dedicated to ITGP. Other titles published by ITGP that may be of interest include:

- IT Governance An International Guide to Data Security and ISO27001/ISO27002

  www.itgovernance.co.uk/shop/p-772.aspx

- Information Security A Practical Guide

  www.itgovernance.co.uk/shop/p-1701.aspx

ITG Resources

- CyberWar, CyberTerror, CyberCrime and CyberActivism

  www.itgovernance.co.uk/shop/p-511.aspx

We also offer a range of off-the-shelf toolkits that give comprehensive, customisable documents to help users create the specific documentation they need to properly implement a management system or standard. Written by experienced practitioners and based on the latest best practice, ITGP toolkits can save months of work for organisations working towards compliance with a given standard.

Please visit *www.itgovernance.co.uk/shop/c-129-toolkits.aspx* to see our full range of toolkits.

Books and tools published by IT Governance Publishing (ITGP) are available from all business booksellers and the following websites:

www.itgovernance.eu   *www.itgovernanceusa.com*

www.itgovernance.in   *www.itgovernancesa.co.za*

www.itgovernance.asia.

Newsletter

You can stay up to date with the latest developments across the whole spectrum of IT governance subject matter, including risk management, information security, ITIL and IT service management, project governance, compliance and so much more, by subscribing to our newsletter.

Simply visit our subscription centre and select your preferences: *www.itgovernance.co.uk/newsletter.aspx*.

Lightning Source UK Ltd.
Milton Keynes UK
UKOW05f1909050617

302754UK00015B/649/P